How to Handle Hard-to-Handle Preschoolers

This book is dedicated to my son and business partner, Marty Appelbaum. We started our company, Appelbaum Training Institute, in our garages with a dream of helping those who work with young children. His dedication and humor as he works and his love for early childhood audiences and what we do are a constant source of support and inspiration to me and to all those he reaches. Thank you, Marty. You are a man of integrity, wisdom, and kindness, and what more could anyone ask for in a son and a business partner?

A Guide for Early Childhood Educators

How to Handle Hard-to-Handle Preschoolers

Maryln Appelbaum

A JOINT PUBLICATION

 CORWIN PRESS
A SAGE Company

 ATi

For information:

Corwin Press
A SAGE Company
2455 Teller Road
Thousand Oaks, California 91320
www.corwinpress.com

SAGE Ltd.
1 Oliver's Yard
55 City Road
London, EC1Y 1SP
United Kingdom

SAGE India Pvt. Ltd.
B 1/I 1 Mohan Cooperative
 Industrial Area
Mathura Road, New Delhi 110 044
India

SAGE Asia-Pacific Pte. Ltd.
33 Pekin Street #02-01
Far East Square
Singapore 048763

Printed in the United States of America.

Library of Congress Cataloging-in-Publication Data

Appelbaum, Maryln.
How to handle hard-to-handle preschoolers : a guide for early
childhood educators / Maryln Appelbaum.
        p. cm.
"A joint publication with the Appelbaum Training Institute."
 Includes bibliographical references and index.
ISBN 978-1-4129-7002-0 (cloth)
ISBN 978-1-4129-7003-7 (pbk.)
1. Children with disabilities—Education (Early childhood) 2. Problem children—Behavior
modification. 3. Behavior disorders in children—Treatment.
I. Appelbaum Training Institute. II. Title.
  LC4019.3.A67 2009
  371.9'0472—dc22
                              2008037559

This book is printed on acid-free paper.

09 10 11 12 13 10 9 8 7 6 5 4 3 2

Acquisitions Editor: Jessica Allan
Editorial Assistant: Joanna Coelho
Production Editor: Appingo Publishing Services
Cover Designer: Rose Storey
Graphic Designer: Karine Hovsepian

Contents

List of Figures

Foreword

Maryln Appelbaum is a remarkable woman. Many of you do not know that she was a high school dropout. Yes, that's right; she was a high school dropout. She grew up in a home of poverty and chaos, was a student at risk, and became one of the hard-to-handle students she writes about in this book. But she had a determination that helped her succeed in spite of the adversity in her life. She was a teenage mom, had two children, and then beat the odds by returning to school to not only finish her high school education, but also to start collecting university degrees and a teaching certificate.

Her studies and her life were always about children. She earned master's degrees in both education and behavioral science. She completed doctoral studies in education and psychology at two universities. She has worked both as a therapist and as a teacher. She found that her real love was teaching hard-to-reach children, and at one point, she owned three early child care centers and packed them with children who were "special." She earned a reputation for being able to find ways to handle each of those children so that when they left her centers, they had something special within them, a gift of knowing they could succeed. When she started those centers, she did not have children who were labeled ADHD, bipolar, LD, Asperger, autistic, or OCD. Yet many of the children she taught came to her centers because they had been expelled from other early childhood centers and schools. Many had all of the above labels, but in those days, those disorders were not identified. When these children came into her centers, they were viewed as special challenges—challenges that could and would be met successfully.

Maryln, in addition to writing books, speaking, and helping run the Appelbaum Training Institute, writes thoughts for the day that go out to educators around the world. In one of her recent thoughts for the day, she wrote, "You just never know the difference you may make." She then went on to tell the story of a woman whom she had recently seen at a holiday party. The woman said, "You probably don't remember me. My son came to your school. We brought him to you because we felt hopeless. He had been labeled mentally retarded at his other school. They said there was no hope. You found the keys to his learning. You gave him the confidence he needed. We saw that he was not mentally retarded. You showed him how he could learn. My son just finished his last year at college. He is now a chemist. I want to thank you."

That is just one of the countless ways Maryln has helped others, which is also what makes this book unique. This book is not only packed with strategies for success, but it is filled with Maryln's stories that are success stories—stories that you will identify with, stories that will motivate you to use the strategies in your classrooms. It is a book filled with hope as well as strategies. She believes that with the help of a caring teacher, children can "beat the odds."

This book is unique because it takes the different special needs of children and offers strategy-based techniques on how to handle those needs and those children. It is a book that will benefit not only preschool teachers but all people who work with children, including doctors, psychologists, social workers, counselors, and administrators of early childhood centers and preschools. The book will also benefit parents. It is more than a book on behavior management and discipline; it is a book on how to connect with every child. It incorporates psychological as well as educational strategies that can totally transform your classroom and the way you teach.

I want to share with you one more story, and it is a personal one. Maryln Appelbaum is my mother, and I am one of her success stories. I struggled in school and was a challenge to teach. Most of my teachers gave up on me. One went so far as to tell my parents that I would never do well in school. I would never make higher than a C and would never be able to attend college. My mother didn't share this information with me and instead vowed to prove to me that I could achieve anything in life that I wanted. In fact, she taught me that I could help others instead of feeling helpless. She taught me to lead instead of needing to be led. She instilled in me the love of teaching. She is an important voice in the lives of hundreds of thousands of educators across the globe. This book is most certainly the best guide of its kind ever written.

—Marty Appelbaum

Preface

It was the '90s, and I was doing teacher training and early childhood training all over the country on behavior management and discipline. Everywhere I went teachers were all talking about the number of children in their classes who had been diagnosed with attention-deficit/hyperactivity disorder (ADHD). They said they had children who could not sit still, children who fidgeted, and children who could not pay attention. They pleaded for help. I resolved to learn all I could on this topic. I did lots of research, contacted other authors, and attended conferences on ADHD conducted by psychologists and psychiatrists. I even contacted drug companies to find out more about the research on the drugs to treat ADHD. In the midst of all this research, I was able to learn firsthand about ADHD through the diagnosis of two close family members. Once I felt ready, I wrote a seminar called "Succeeding With Students with ADHD." We had standing-room-only crowds of educators all wanting to know what they could do. The more I traveled, the more I learned as I taught. Everyone wanted to share their stories about their experiences with ADHD.

Another topic, learning disorders (LD), was developed in the same way. A very dear family member had LD, so I had already researched this disorder, plus I had many children in my own early childhood centers that had difficulties learning. So many children have both ADHD and LD that it naturally followed that LD came to be included in seminars on ADHD.

As I traveled around the country giving seminars on ADHD and LD, preschool teachers started asking about children with anger management issues. They said they had never before had so many children who had tantrums and raged. I did background research and wrote another seminar, "Succeeding With Angry, Defiant, and ODD Students." It, too, was a huge success.

At that time, very few children were diagnosed with PDD—pervasive developmental disorder; however, numbers soon increased for this as well as for bipolar disorder. Bullying also became a problem in schools. Moreover, preschool teachers complained that more and more children were misbehaving. They couldn't sit still, constantly chattered, complained, tattled, and were disruptive. I wrote a new seminar called "How to Handle the Hard-to-Handle Student." It incorporated ADHD, PDD, anger, defiance, ODD, bullying, bipolar disorder, Tourette syndrome, obsessive compulsive disorder, and other tough classroom issues like disruptive students, tattling, constant chatter in the classroom, and classroom conflicts. Once again, teachers flocked to these seminars to learn strategies for handling these children. National associations for teachers and therapists asked me to speak at their conferences on these topics.

This book is the result of the demand for strategies to handle these hard-to-handle preschoolers. The strategies are all designed to help you help your preschool children

- Develop the ability to self-regulate whether or not an adult is present.
- Learn how to problem solve.
- Learn positive alternative behaviors to replace negative behaviors.
- Learn how to handle their emotions appropriately.
- Succeed not only in the classroom but also in life.

Each chapter begins with an explanation for each disorder or behavioral problem so that you can have a better understanding as well as recognize the symptoms. Many strategies follow the explanation. The reason there are many strategies is because no one strategy works for all children. Every child is unique. What works for one child will not necessarily work for another child, and what works for one child at one time may not work later at another time.

There is also no one strategy that works for all teachers. Teachers all have their own teaching styles, and what is comfortable for one teacher may not be comfortable for another. Each classroom is like a box of crayons. Each color crayon has its own unique beauty. Some of the crayons in the box may be shorter, some longer; some may have pointy tips, and some have been used so much that they are rounded. When these crayons are used together, they create a beautiful drawing. Your classroom is the same. Every child is like one of those crayons—unique and special. This book is packed with strategies to help you open up that crayon box and create your classroom—to unite your class into a "we" instead of a "me."

This book is filled with stories of children and their teachers to illustrate the strategies. I have changed all of the names of these wonderful "crayons" to protect their identities. I sincerely hope that you will find this book as valuable as have the tens of thousands of people who have taken the training on which it is based. They have all taught me so much.

Acknowledgments

Thank you to the enthusiastic team at Corwin Press, starting with my editor, Jessica Allan. Jessica, it has been so much fun conceiving this idea together, working with you, and getting your creative input on this book and everything related to it. Special thanks to Allyson Sharp, for your special brand of enthusiasm and commitment to education and educational books. Thank you to the entire Corwin Press team. You have helped make it fun for me to write this book.

Thank you to the tens of thousands of preschool teachers and administrators who have attended our Appelbaum Training Institute seminars and always have been a constant source of feedback and support. You inspired me to learn all I could so I could help you, and watching you all succeed has been a gift in my life.

The other great gift in my life has been my own children and grandchildren. I am so blessed to have you all: Marty, Carol, Ciara, Tobi, Sean, Beth, and Gary. Your love fills my heart, mind, and soul.

Thank you to my friends. You all are a tremendous support in my life for which I am so grateful.

PUBLISHER'S ACKNOWLEDGMENTS

Corwin Press wishes to acknowledge the following peer reviewers for their editorial insight and guidance:

Sandra Kraynok, NBCT
Kindergarten Teacher
Rock Cave Elementary School
Rock Cave, WV

Pamela L. Opel, NBCT
Science Curriculum Specialist
Gulfport School District
Gulfport, MS

Jill J. Simmons-Stemple, NBCT
Author of *Stepping Today Into Pre-K*
Preschool Teacher
Upshur County Schools/Head Start
Buckhannon, WV

Lois Wachtel
CEO and President
Creative Beginning Steps
Early Childhood Workshops
Boca Raton, FL

About the Author

**Maryln Appelbaum** is well known internationally as an authority on children, education, and families. She has master's degrees in both psychology and education and has completed her doctoral studies in both fields. She has worked as a teacher, an administrator, and a therapist and has been an educational consul-tant throughout the United States. She has written more than 30 how-to books geared toward educators and parents. She has been interviewed on television and radio talk shows and has been quoted in newspapers, including *USA Today*.

She owns a seminar training company, Appelbaum Training Institute, with her son, Marty Appelbaum, and they and their speakers train 50,000 preschool educators every year throughout the United States.

Maryln's influence is felt daily all over the world with her thoughts for the day that go out to thousands of educators via e-mail. Her strategies have been successfully implemented in schools around the world. Not a day goes by that someone does not contact her at the Appelbaum Training Institute to thank her. Those thank yous come from teachers, administrators, parents, and students whose lives have been shaped by Maryln.

Her books and her talks are strategy based. She does not believe in a "one-size-fits-all" solution and instead provides multiple strategies to reflect the diversity that exists in both children and teachers. She believes that there is a way to help every child succeed. She is enthusiastic, dynamic, dedicated, and caring: a one-of-a-kind difference maker for the world.

How to Handle Children Who Are Disruptive

1

Children need encouragement like roses need sunshine.
                                        —Maryln Appelbaum

There are many ways children can disrupt the classroom. They may tattle, complain, blurt out, chatter, get into fights, and insist on having what they want, when they want it. Each type of disruption needs separate strategies and skills. This chapter will give you the skills you need to handle these hard-to-handle children and hard-to-handle situations.

SKILL ONE: HOW TO HANDLE TATTLING

Janette was a brand new preschool teacher. Little Mikey was in her class. He had huge dark eyes, dark curly hair, and a wonderful smile. When he came in each morning, he ran over to Janette and gave her a huge hug. The problem was that he also ran over to her at least once or twice an hour with a tattle about a classmate. Tattling is a very disruptive behavior (Gartrell, 2007). Children who tattle disrupt the routine and the consistency of the classroom. Tattling is detrimental to promoting harmony and cooperation between children.

The origins of tattling are generally in the home. Children learn that when they tattle on a sibling, a friend, or another family member, that person gets in trouble. Children who tattle get sympathy and attention for the tattle. They also learn that when they have problems, adults will step in and solve their problems. They come to preschool and tattle for the same reasons. You cannot help what happens in the home, but you can help what happens in the classroom. Tattling can be stopped.

The first step in stopping tattling is to teach children the difference between tattling and reporting. Tattling is to get someone in trouble. Reporting is when a child gets help for someone. Role-play tattling and reporting and have children tell you which one is being used.

- Jason tells you that Todd is hitting Scott in the playground and that Scott is bleeding. Is this an example of reporting or tattling?
  This is an example of reporting. Jason appears to be trying to get help for Scott.
- Tonya tells you that Sasha does not want play with her. Is this a report or a tattle?
  This is an example of tattling. Tonya appears to be trying to get Sasha into trouble. No one is getting hurt.

Have children give you other examples of reporting and tattling. The more they practice, the better they will get at recognizing the difference between the two.

Strategies for Success for Tattling

Staying Calm

Remain calm when you hear tattles. When children see that you get upset, it actually reinforces the tattling behavior. They think this is a way that they can always get attention and sympathy. The more sympathy they get, the more they will engage in tattling. Take a few deep breaths and stay calm. Remember, the more you react, the more they act!

Tootles Curriculum

Tattling can become contagious. When children see that one child gets attention for tattling, soon they may all start doing it. This may be a sign that children need attention, but in more positive ways. An excellent way to stop tattling in its tracks is to set up a "tootles" curriculum. Tootles are kind statements that children say about others (Skinner, Cashwell, & Skinner, 2000). They are the opposite of tattles. Give children examples of tootles. "Kathy helped Kenny when he dropped his backpack and everything fell out." "Alfie helped Elma put away the blocks."

Have a special tootles time each day. It is a good concluding group activity. Children report all the good things others did. Every time you hear a tootle during circle time or during the day, add a paper clip to a tootles glass jar. It needs to be clear glass jar so the children can see the effects of their tootles as the jar is filled. When the jar is filled with paper clips, the class has a tootles party. Bring in a special treat and encourage them on that day to tell each other lots of tootles so everyone leaves happy.

This is an effective strategy because it teaches children to say nice statements about each other rather than negative ones. The more they get focused on saying positives, the more the negatives fall by the wayside. It creates a different positive climate in the classroom.

Thanks

A simple and effective strategy for handling tattling is to hear the tattle and then calmly say, "Thanks." Display very little emotion. Children learn from this that tattling gets no real sympathy or attention. They learn to handle their own problems and not get attention from trying to get another child into trouble.

"Sounds Like"

This is an excellent strategy for handling tattling. It acknowledges the emotions children have when they tattle, but does not reinforce the behavior. When you use this technique, you respond to the feeling the child has. You are using empathetic listening without getting actively involved. When Kenny comes to you and says, "Joshie said a bad word," respond by saying, "Sounds like you're upset." Kenny feels acknowledged and heard, yet you did not get involved in resolving the issue.

Tattle Sandwich

A sandwich is composed of two slices of bread with something in the middle. A tattle sandwich is composed of two compliments (the slices of bread), and the tattle in the middle. If children want to tattle, they have to first say something nice about the other child. Then they say the tattle. After saying the tattle, they say something else nice about the other child. This forces them to think in a whole new manner about the children that they are trying to get into trouble. They are now looking for good things to say about these children. Here's an example: Meagan approached Ms. Janie, her teacher, and said, "Stephanie has on a pretty dress." This is the first part of the statement—one of the slices of "bread." Then she said, "She won't share her toys with me." That was her tattle. She paused and thought about the other "slice of bread" that had to be nice. She said, "Stephanie gave me one of her crackers yesterday." The great thing about teaching children to use tattle sandwiches is that it teaches them to focus on the positives about each other, which minimizes tattling.

Tattle Time

If tattling is a real issue in your classroom, set up a special time each day when children get to tell their tattles. They cannot tell them before that time. By the time tattle time rolls around, they typically have forgotten all about the issue that had them upset in the first place. If they do remember the issue, they have to state it in the form of a tattle sandwich, saying two positives as well as the tattle.

Tattle Bucket

Have a special small bucket called the tattle bucket. Make name cards for each child. Use colored index cards for the name cards. Write each child's name on a separate name card, and then add a unique sticker to each card. The different stickers help children who cannot read their names identify their cards because they recognize their stickers. When children have a tattle, instead of disrupting the class, they get their name card and put it into the tattle bucket. Look in the bucket at varying times during the day. If you see a name card, go to the child and say, "I see you have your name card in the tattle bucket. What would you like to tell me?" Many times, children will have forgotten all about the tattle.

Tattle Ear

There are some children who just like to talk about others. They are not reporting. They are tattling, telling one negative after another. Their goal is to get others in trouble. When children start to tell you tattles like these and are rambling on, have them go tell it to the "ear." Draw an ear and hang the drawing on the wall. Explain that this is the tattle ear, and they are to tell their tattles to the ear. Recently, I went into a preschool and saw one of the children, Maria, walk up to the wall where there was a tattle ear and stand there telling her tattle to the ear. When she finished, she went and rejoined her friends playing in the dramatic play center. She did this all very calmly. It was adorable to watch.

Teach Alternatives to Tattling

Children sometimes do not mean to tattle about someone else. They do it because they are having a problem with another child and just don't know any other way to handle the problem. Teach them other methods to handle the situation. This is not the same as telling them how to handle the situation. When you tell them exactly how to handle situations, they are not learning to think for themselves or to take responsibility for their choices. Teaching them involves explaining different alternatives for the troublesome situation. For example, Lori approaches her teacher and says, "Cindi is taking too long." Ms. Jenkins says, "You could say, 'Cindi, I would like a turn now,' or you could do something else until Cindi is finished. Which do you prefer?"

SKILL TWO: HOW TO HANDLE COMPLAINING

Complaining is similar to, but different from, tattling. It is similar in that children have formed a pattern of negative statements to get attention. However, it is different because the complaints may not be about other people, but about situations. It is also different because children who frequently complain may develop victim mentalities. This occurs when children feel powerless about many issues. Children can begin to believe that everything bad happens to them. They complain about everything (Parish & Mahoney, 2006). They say, "I can't," and actually stop trying to do things. They say they can't do a drawing. They can't play in centers. They can't do a partner activity. They give constant negative excuses. They complain that their classmates do not like them. It's important to break this negative pattern of behavior. Children need to develop confidence in themselves. They need to learn their strengths and maximize them.

Strategies for Success for Complaining

"I Can't" to "I Can"

This is a really powerful strategy to teach children to say "I can," rather than "I can't." Begin by asking children all the things they cannot do. Write separate lists for each child. Read their lists aloud to them individually. Now it is time to have an "I can't" ceremony. Give them their lists and have the children tear them up. Then they toss them into the wastebasket. The goal is to get rid of all the "I can'ts."

Next, get a dictionary. Find the word "impossible." Tell the children that impossible means something that they can't do. Tell them you are going to scratch out the word "impossible" and then do it.

Tell children stories of people who refused to believe in the word "impossible." Tell them your own stories of how you didn't give up when things got rough. Tell them about others. Beethoven was deaf, yet he composed beautiful music. Einstein could not talk until he was 4 years old and had a very difficult time learning in school, but he went on to become famous for his theories. Tell the children what these brilliant individuals have in common is the fact that they never gave up. They never listened to the word "impossible." They believed, instead, that everything was possible.

Now the children are ready for the last step, and that is to make lists of all the things they would like to do that they previously thought were impossible. Have them each dictate to you all the things they can do. Put each "I can" on a separate sheet of paper. Have the children color each "I can" and put them all together so they each have their own individual "I can" book. Put the books in the book corner. Label the books with each child's name and unique sticker.

Connect

One of the most important strategies for all children—those who complain, those who are shy and withdrawn, or those who are disruptive—is to connect (Parish & Mahoney, 2006). Every child needs to feel a sense of belonging. Children do not care how much you know until they know how much you care. When you take time to connect, it totally changes the dynamics of working with even the toughest child. Instead of constant bickering, nagging, and becoming frustrated, you will instead develop a completely new relationship with the children.

One-to-One Meetings This is a great way to connect. It takes some time, but it is so worth it. The truth is that your tough, disruptive children already are taking up precious time in a negative way. This is a positive way to take time that will save time later. Set aside a special time to meet with your toughest child daily for three consecutive weeks. The meeting needs to be for three uninterrupted minutes. Schedule the meeting for a time when you can put your entire focus on the child.

This is not a time for you to do the talking. It is about getting to know the child. Start by explaining that you want this special time together to get to know the child better. Bring up a topic that you think will interest the child. If you are unsure, start with a topic that all children are interested in—a favorite television show, a favorite movie star, or a hobby.

Power Listening When the child begins to talk, use power listening. Power listening is listening in a way so that children want to talk. It is very effective. Sit so that you are both facing each other. It is best to be on the same level. As the child talks, nod your head to indicate that you are listening. Every now and then, say, "Really?" or, "Hmmm." If the child describes something with lots of emotional impact, say, "Sounds like . . ." plus the emotion. For example, "Sounds like that made you angry." Your goal is for the child to keep talking. At the end of the time, thank the child and say that you look forward to doing this again.

At first, children will not understand what you are doing. They will wonder why you are doing it; however, after a while, they will grow to like their special time with you. You will build a bond that is enduring.

SKILL THREE: HOW TO HANDLE CONSTANT CHATTER

Our company, the Appelbaum Training Institute, conducted an online survey that listed many disruptive behaviors, including constant chatter. Teachers were asked to choose the most disruptive. The number one disruptive behavior that was chosen was constant chatter! There is a difference between the quiet buzz and fun talking that takes place in the classroom when children are playing or working together on a project and chatter (Bausman, Bent, & Collister, 1999). Chatter occurs when you are trying to give the children directions, and they are not paying attention. It can also get very loud. Chatter in the classroom is disruptive for the entire class. When one child starts talking, it becomes contagious for other children to be talking, and soon the entire classroom is talking. It's important to stop chatter before it reaches this point.

Strategies for Success for Constant Chatter

Taking Charge

Start by taking charge of the classroom. Someone needs to be in charge. If you do not take charge, the children will. Walk confidently. Speak with poise and confidence and believe in yourself and your ability to control the classroom. Children can feel when you are frightened and unsure of yourself. You may have to practice speaking in front of a mirror until your voice is strong, firm, and filled with positive expectations. Do this over and over again. You can also tape record yourself while talking to children. Afterward, as you listen to the tapes, ask yourself, "Would I listen to me? What can I do better?" Practice, practice, and practice some more.

Fun Atmosphere

The more fun you have, the more fun children will have. They will want to pay attention to you because they are excited to see what you will do next. Your enthusiasm is more contagious than a cold. It is infectious. The truth is that any mood you have is contagious, so it is really important that your mood is filled with joy for teaching.

Silence Game

This is a method first devised by Maria Montessori when she was working with young children in the slums of San Lorenzo, Italy. She used it to teach them the power of silence (Bettmann, 2000). It worked then, and it works now. Here's how to do it. Tell the children that you will be asking them to close their eyes and listen. It will be for less than a minute. When they open their eyes, ask them to name all the sounds they heard.

They generally will hear the air conditioning or heating vent, other children breathing, and noise in the hallway. The next day, do it again for a few seconds longer. Every day, do it longer and longer. It is amazing the sounds they start to hear that they never heard before. This game sets the tone for teaching children the value of silence. Some of them never experience silence. They go home, and their television sets are always on. The television is even on when they go to sleep. They have grown accustomed to noise rather than silence. That is one of the reasons they chatter. With this game, you are teaching them to be still and enjoy the silence. It is a skill that will last their entire lifetimes.

Talking Without Sound

Have a special time each day when children can talk to each other without words. They make gestures, but no words. Children look forward to this special time that is generally held at the end of the day as a fun time. You can use it at other times too, whenever you think the noise level is getting loud.

Silence Sign

Take a brightly colored 8½ by 11 sheet of cardstock and print the word "silence" on it. Show it to the children. Tell them that it says "silence." Explain that silence means to be totally still, to not talk, and to not move. Tell them that every time you hold up the silence sign, they are to get into the "pause position." There are four parts to the pause position:

1. Stop talking
2. Put eyes on teacher
3. Put feet together
4. Fold arms in front of chest

Demonstrate how to do this. Hold up the silence sign and have the class practice getting into the pause position. During regular class time, hold up the silence sign. Some children will not see it, so start speaking quietly and calmly to those who saw the sign as you continue holding the sign, "I am holding the silence sign, and Jenny sees it and is in the pause position. Now Tomas sees it and is in the pause position." Name a few more names until all of the children are standing quietly. Thank the children and give them some instructions.

This is an extremely effective strategy for cutting chatter. One day many years ago, I was teaching a group of 4-year-olds when I received a phone call that there was a tornado warning, and the preschool was directly in the predicted path of the tornado. I needed to get the children into the hallway where they would be protected. All of the other rooms had windows, and there were no basements because it was in Houston. I held up the silence sign, and the children immediately got into the pause position. I told them to walk very quietly into the hallway and then quietly sit down. They did. When they were in the hallway, we sang songs until the danger passed. The children had a great time and never even knew there was danger. Children like gimmicks, and the silence sign with the pause position are fun for them to do and a great way to stop chatter.

Chatter Box

Use a music box to keep track of time lost to chatter. When chatter begins, the music starts. When chatter stops, the lid on the music box goes down. At the end of class, play the unused portion of music. This is the time available for free talk. Children learn to save their talk so they can have a longer, more meaningful free talk time. If you cannot find a music box, you can use a song on a CD.

Anchor Activities

When children have nothing to do, they may get bored. To entertain themselves they may engage in inappropriate behavior. Have fun anchor activities for when children finish what they are doing and are waiting to see what will happen next. Anchor activities are activities that fill up time in an appropriate way (Hipsky, 2007). Examples of anchor activities are puzzles, fun reading books, and quiet games. Anchor activities provide a way to keep students busy having fun.

SKILL FOUR: HOW TO HANDLE BLURTING OUT

Blurting out occurs when children loudly say whatever it is they are thinking (Charney, 1998). It also occurs when they raise their hands to get the attention of teachers. They wave their hands frantically in the air as they yell, "Teacher, teacher!"

Strategies for Success for Blurting Out

Two-Hand Rule

The two-hand rule is a great way to solve problems with blurting out. Teach children that whenever they raise their hand, their other hand goes over their mouth. The hand over the mouth is a reminder to keep it closed until called upon. Have children practice using the two-hand rule. Ask them a question and have them raise their hand to answer you. During class time, if children forget to use the two-hand rule, gently but firmly remind them.

Avoiding Reinforcing Negative Behaviors

It's important to monitor your own behavior during blurt-outs. Do you call on children who blurt out? If you do, you are reinforcing the behavior that you wish to end. Every time you call on them when they blurt out, you are saying, "It's OK to blurt out. That's a good way to get attention." Avoid putting your attention on behaviors you do not want to reoccur. Whatever you put your attention on will expand and grow. Place it on negative behaviors, and they will expand and grow. Place it on positive behaviors, and they will expand and grow.

Hand Signals

There are times when children really do need to get your attention, and they need to do it quickly. If they need something that is urgent, have them raise their entire hand in a fist. The fist means that it is an emergency and they need your attention immediately. This is a great way for them to tell you when they need to go to the bathroom.

SKILL FIVE: HOW TO HANDLE TALKING BACK

When children talk back it is not only disruptive, but it is also disrespectful. It sets a tone for other children to become disrespectful. It is something that has to be stopped before it increases.

Strategies for Success for Talking Back

Appointment Cards

It is important that you show children you are the one who determines how and when disruptions will be handled, rather than the children.

Explain ahead of time to the entire class that appointment cards are cards that set up meetings with you at a special time during the day. When a child starts talking back or is disruptive, give the child an appointment card and explain that you will be meeting with him or her later: "Here is your appointment card for after circle time." Resume teaching. By the time of the appointment, the child will be calmer. During the appointment, teach children other ways to ask for what they want in a courteous manner. Have them role-play asking for what they want.

Figure 1.1 Appointment Card

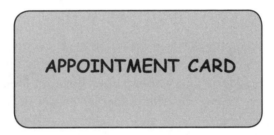

Use Power Talk

There are special ways to talk to children so they listen the first time. Use power talk. There are several components to power talk.

Words—"I Need" Statements   The words you use are very important. "I need" statements demonstrate respect for children, yet are assertive. Here's an example of an "I need" statement:

"*Graham, (pause) I need you, (pause) to stop, (pause) now.*"

The first word is always the child's name followed by a pause. Then say, "I need you," and pause again. Now say what it is you want the child to do. If it is urgent, add the word "now." The pauses are very important. As you pause, the child hears the emphasis in your voice of what needs to be done.

Squat   Squat down as you speak so that you are on the same level with the child, about two to three feet apart. It is important to not be too close or it may seem threatening to the child.

You also don't want to be too far away. It's important to never speak across the room. When you speak across the room, children learn from observing to do the same thing, and soon they start speaking across the room, raising their voices to other children.

Voice Tone   Use a low, deep voice. Often teachers have their voices get louder and louder as they speak. Make sure to have your voice get lower and lower. The lower you speak, the more emphasis there is in your voice.

Speak With Confidence   The more you believe that children will listen to you when you speak, the more they will listen. They can tell when you are confident and they can tell when you are not. Practice, practice, and practice some more. This is an extremely effective technique, but it only works with lots of practice.

SKILL SIX: HOW TO HANDLE POWER STRUGGLES

Power struggles are exhausting. A power struggle occurs when children want their way, and they hold out until they get what they want. It's a learned behavior. Children learn that if they hold out long enough, they can always get what they want. They generally do this not only in interactions with teachers, but also with their families. Family members typically describe these children as being strong willed. They are strong in determination. This is an asset. It's important to not squelch their strength, but to teach them to be respectful of others.

Power struggles occur when children want what they want, when they want it, and the teacher wants them to do something else (Ferko, 2005). I can still remember at the beginning of my teaching career when this happened to me. I engaged in all the typical behaviors that did not work. I ignored the child and hoped the problem would go away. Sometimes, I yelled. Other times, I argued with children, and they argued back. Eventually one of us had to give in, and I'm embarrassed to say often I was that person. I would just become so worn out that I gave in. As soon as I did this, of course, the child learned, "If I hold out long enough, I can always get what I want." The power struggles continued and continued with each one taking longer and longer to resolve (see Figure 1.2).

Strategies for Success for Power Struggles

Appelbaum Rule of Three

It took a while, but I finally understood that I could not give in. I also realized what I now call the "Appelbaum Rule of Three." Every time you give in, you ensure that the child will engage in another power struggle at least three more times. That is because the child has won and has learned to hold out longer than you. The child will be convinced that this time will be no exception and will continue to struggle with you.

Figure 1.2 Power Struggles Cycle

Power Struggles Cycle	
Child's Behavior	Engages in inappropriate behavior Makes inappropriate request
Teacher's Reaction	Ignores Argues Yells
Child's Behavior	Additional inappropriate request or behavior
Teacher's Reaction	Ignores Argues Yells
Child's Behavior	Additional inappropriate request or behavior
Teacher's Reaction	Gives in
Child's Reaction	"I won." "This works."

There are really no winners when this happens. Children may think they have won, but they have really lost. They have lost because they think they have learned something about the real world. In the real world, they cannot always have what they want, when they want it. That is not how it works.

One day, many years ago, I was on an airplane flying to give a seminar. I got into a conversation with a flight attendant. She was a very attractive, perky, 23-year-old woman. She asked me what I was doing because I had my notes out in front of me to prepare for the seminar. I told her that I was going to give a seminar on behavior management of children. She said, "Please tell my story." She then proceeded to tell me about her life. She said that as a child, she got everything she wanted, when she wanted it. She said she would cry and have tantrums if she didn't get what she wanted. Her parents always gave in. She said that she started to have problems in her relationships in elementary school. She expected other students to also give her what she wanted. When they did not, she became angry and friendships ended. She said that she had recently been engaged to a man she loved very much. She said she followed the same pattern with him, and he broke the engagement. To top it all off, she said that her parents had cancelled her credit cards this past year. They wanted her to make it on her own. She said she had no idea how to do that. She had taken this job, but she did not know if she would be able to keep it because her behaviors were so deeply entrenched. She ended her story by pleading with me, "Tell them my story. Tell them so they know not to do this with children."

I do not know what happened to this young woman. One can only hope that she somehow made her life more successful. Her story is an inspiration to not give in to children all the time, to help them learn to be respectful, and to teach them skills that will last their entire lives.

Two Positive Choices

Typically, when there is a power struggle, teachers do offer choices. However, the choice is between a positive choice and a negative choice. It becomes a threat. "Do this or _____ will happen." This serves to make children rebel even more and hold out longer. When you offer two positive choices, children generally forget about their struggle and choose one of the two. "You can go to the reading center now or you can work at the art easel. Which do you prefer?"

Children still feel powerful. They are still in control of what they do; however, it is now between the limits you have provided.

Delaying

When children are extremely emotional about something, it is often wise to use the delaying tactic. This gives both of you time to cool down and think more rationally. Say, "I can see you are really upset. I am too. I need to talk about this later. We can do it after circle time this morning or after lunch. Which do you prefer?"

Children still feel empowered because, once again, they have been asked to make a choice. However, once again, you are in charge as you delay the conversation. It's important to remember that children really need someone to be in charge. Yes, they want freedom, but they are happiest when it is within limits. This gives them the structure they so badly need. Too much freedom can result in chaos for them. It is like going to a department store that has a sale. You walk in and see tables all over saying "50–80 percent off today." There are people pulling and poking all the products on the tables in their struggle to find bargains. It is chaos. Even as you reach in to look for your own bargain, you know that you would prefer to find the bargain another way—a way that had structure rather than chaos.

Changing the Frame

When children engage in a power struggle, they get stuck continuing the struggle until they get what they want. Sometimes, by the time they get what they want, they do not really even care about what it was. Instead, it is about winning. Change this mental frame by distracting the child. Say something that is completely and totally different from what you both are talking about. For example, one day 4-year-old Brandon was trying to get his teacher, Mrs. Carlton, in a power struggle. Mrs. Carlton suddenly turned to Brandon and said, "Oh my gosh! I think I left my garage door open this morning. I can't believe that it may be open. I wonder how I can get the garage door shut. My husband is at work, and I'm here. Oh my gosh!" Brandon stopped in his tracks and looked at Mrs. Carlton with a look that said, "Are you kidding?" She went on talking about her garage door, and Brandon walked away, forgetting all about the power struggle.

Mrs. Engle had her own way of handling power struggles. Mrs. Engle loved to sing. She would break out in a song in the middle of teaching. Her children loved her. She would make up words to songs to tie into teaching any concept. She did not plan the words ahead. She just got up there and taught and sang. She had complete command of the class's attention. She was fun and entertaining as she taught. Raul was one of her students and was very strong willed. He got into trouble and had power struggles with all other adults, but he never got into trouble in Mrs. Engle's class. When asked about how she handled Raul, she said, "I sing. Whenever he begins to become argumentative, I either get the whole class singing a fun song, or I just look at him and start singing something." Mrs. Engle burst into song, "Not right now, Raul, not right now. Later, later, later. You can sing with me, Raul, later, later, later." Raul always joined her in song, and they smiled and laughed, and the power struggle never happened. She had changed the frame with a song.

SKILL SEVEN: HOW TO HANDLE CHILDREN'S CONFLICTS

Conflict in early childhood, as in adulthood, is inevitable. Conflict occurs when two or more people have different views on a similar topic, and they not only disagree but also try to convince the other person that their views are the correct ones. They confront each other often in unpleasant ways (Turnuklu, 2007). Instead, they need to learn to "carefront." "Carefrontation" occurs when two or more people still disagree, but discuss their disagreement in a caring way with each other.

Conflict occurs in young children for various reasons. Sometimes it occurs because children lack social and communication interaction skills. One child may be struggling to say something, and it comes across to the other child as hostile or threatening. As soon as this occurs, the second child then retaliates by becoming hostile and even more threatening. Before you know it, a huge fight has sprouted from a really insignificant occurrence that became magnified.

Another reason that conflict may occur is when a child enters the classroom with displaced anger. Ethan was one of those children. He came into his preschool classroom one morning with a chip on his shoulder. What no one knew is that the night before, his dad had left his mom. His mom had told Ethan that it was his fault. She said, "If only you had been better, he would not have left." Ethan felt like he was a bad child. He came into his preschool the next day angry and hostile. When he and Gregie were working together in the block area, Ethan started picking on Gregie. Nothing Gregie could do was right. Gregie was a patient and quiet child, but Ethan kept picking on him. Gregie got angrier and angrier, and soon he said some things back to Ethan. The conflict was on.

If Ethan had been able to come into preschool and talk about his feelings, this could have been prevented. Instead, he came into school angry and hostile. His feelings escalated as the day went on, as he kept thinking about what had occurred the night before.

Strategies for Success for Children's Conflicts

When children and adults get angry, they confront each other and often say unpleasant things that they may later regret. They may become aggressive and even combative. Instead of confronting each other, it is better to "carefront" each other. In a "carefrontation" there is still a lack of agreement about a situation; however, the skills that are used to resolve the situation are caring skills.

Conflict resolution in general is not something that comes naturally. It is a skill that needs to be developed. Children need to learn this skill, which will help them throughout their entire lives. It will also help make your classroom a better place, a safer place, and a place where children treat each other with respect. Take lots of time to teach this skill. Start teaching it at the beginning of the school year and take time to periodically review it.

"I Need" Statements

Typically when young children are mad at each other, they make lots of "you" statements. They say "You did . . . and you did. . . . " "You" statements are accusatory and are almost guaranteed to cause the other child to become upset and hostile. This promotes confrontation rather than carefrontation.

Teach children to use "I need" statements (Heydenberk & Heydenberk, 2007). Instead of accusing another child of an inappropriate behavior, they say, "I need," and ask for what they want. Then they always say, "Is that OK with you?" If the other child says, "No," the first child says, "OK," and goes on to do something else. This is a strategy that has to be rehearsed with the children. Earlier I talked about using "power talk." Children will copy you. That is one of the best ways to teach "I need" statements. You are always a role model. They are watching you at all times and learning.

Peace Table

Set up a small table with three seats in the classroom. One seat will be for you, and the other two seats will be for children who are fighting. When children are in conflict, have them go to the peace table to use carefrontation—to talk about it. You will be the mediator. It's important to start not with the accusations of each child, but instead with the end goals. Have a "Peace Wand." This is a small wand you can make using construction paper. Children cannot talk unless they are holding the wand. Have the children take turns holding the wand and asking for what they need. "I need Cody to share the toys." "I need Ethan to say nice things to me." After the children share what they want, have them say one nice thing they like about each other and then shake hands or hug.

I was observing at an early childhood program, making video clips to use in seminars, when two 4-year-old girls got into a fight. I immediately took advantage of the situation so I could videotape it for audiences to see. The school did not have a peace table, so I quickly made one and improvised a wand. I had the children sit opposite each other and say what they needed. It was adorable. They were two little girls and the fighting had become intense before sitting at the peace table. When I asked the children to tell each other something nice they liked about each other, they were each at a loss at first. It was a new concept for them. The first child, Samantha, looked at Emmy, the other little girl, and finally responded, "Pizza." I had no idea what she meant. I said, "Pizza?" with a question mark in my voice. Samantha said, "Emmy loves pizza. I do too. I like that." When it was Emmy's turn, she said, "Candy." Children say the cutest things, and you just never know what they will say. The point is that the children did list something they liked about each other and afterward gave each other big hugs. The conflict was resolved using carefrontation.

Peace Chain

Begin with a box of oval links cut from construction paper. Encourage your class to catch each other in acts of peacemaking. These include children choosing not to fight and children helping others who are upset to feel better. Each time an act of peace is reported, a link describing the act is added to a chain that starts at the ceiling. When the chain touches the floor, hold a celebration.

Role-Plays

Children need to be taught appropriate skills for communication. Do this through role-play. Use puppets to demonstrate social skills, including how to accept "no" for an answer. Have children get into dyads. One partner makes a request. The other partner responds, "No." The first child says, "OK." Have them take turns practicing, repeatedly making new requests, then hearing "no" and responding "OK."

Have them practice both giving and receiving compliments. There are children who have never said a nice word to another child. In fact, they may not have ever said a nice word to another person at home either. Make sure they understand that it has to be sincere. If it is insincere, it feels worse than if nothing was said.

Teach them how to receive compliments. There are children who are more comfortable giving them than receiving them. These children may not feel worthy, or it may just be so foreign to them that they feel strange. Teach them to respond, "Thank you." Have them take turns giving and receiving compliments and responding, "Thank you."

How to Handle Children With Attention-Deficit/ Hyperactivity Disorder

2

ADHD is a "hidden disability."

—Maryln Appelbaum

The first step in working with preschoolers with attention-deficit/ hyperactivity disorder (ADHD) is to understand that this is a real disability. You can't see it as easily as when you see someone wearing a pair of glasses, using a hearing aid, or sitting in a wheelchair; however, it is still very real. It is a disorder that is often invisible, buried beneath what appears to be misbehavior, sloppiness, laziness, and even stubbornness. I call it the hidden disability.

ADHD has been around a long time. Over 100 years ago, the medical community focused on a combination of deficits in attention, learning, motor skills, and motivation (Gillberg, 2003). The name for this combination of deficits changed over the years, and today it has come to be called ADHD. It is the most common mental disorder of childhood (Stolzer, 2007) and affects 7.5 percent of children (Fine, 2002) in the United States. The ADHD diagnosis accounts for 50 percent of the children in child psychiatry clinics in America (Leslie, Weckerly, Plemmons, Landsyerk, & Eastman, 2004). It is a very real disorder.

When I think of an executive, I think of someone who is in charge of a large company. That person performs many functions to organize employees and ensure that the company operates smoothly. The brain also has executive functions—functions to ensure that operations are organized. There are several executive functions that may be affected in children with ADHD (Stearns, Dunham, McIntosh, & Dean, 2004).

A very important executive function is nonverbal memory. This is the child's ability to keep representations—pictures of events—in the mind. These pictures then become part of children's memories. These pictures are very important because they help children picture what will happen if they engage in an action. Preschoolers with ADHD often have a deficit with this executive function, and because they cannot picture what will happen, they act impulsively.

Another very important executive function is working memory (Biederman et al., 2000, as cited by Stearns et al., 2004). Working memory stores and manipulates information to do tasks. Children need working memory to remember the rules of behavior and problem solving. When children have a deficit in working memory, they do not remember to stop engaging in inappropriate behaviors. That is why children with ADHD often engage in the same inappropriate behaviors repeatedly, even though they have experienced consequences. Early childhood teachers have said to me, "I don't understand. They get in trouble every time. Why do they just keep doing it?" It is because it is not in their working memory.

Children with ADHD generally have problems following rules. This is because of another deficit in executive function—self-regulation. Self-regulation is important because this is the function that gives children the self-discipline they need to set goals and work toward those goals. They need this so they can pay attention to tasks, even when they are disinterested, bored, or tired. When this function is operating, they learn to start tasks and complete them. They do not need anyone to look over their shoulders to ensure they are moving toward their goals.

All of these functions are internal. You cannot see these functions, so it is easy to forget they are there. Instead, you may think, "Petey is lazy." "He hates following rules." "He never follows through." "It's in one ear, and out the other." "He loses everything." "I never know what he will do next."

A huge problem is that after a while, children start believing they are not as good as their peers. I met Sherry, an adult with ADHD, while I was giving seminars on ADHD. Sherry told me that even as a very young child, she always felt different from other children. She never fit in with her peers, and she felt like she never could get anything right. As she got older, she compared herself to her older sister who did not have ADHD. Sadly, her parents also compared her to her sister, and Sherry came up short! No one knew she had ADHD. Everyone, both at school and at home, thought she was deliberately not following through when asked to do something.

They thought she was lazy and stubborn and not very smart. Actually, Sherry had an above-average IQ, but it was not readily seen because of her lack of follow-through on assignments and tasks. Unfortunately, no one diagnosed her until late into adulthood. By then, her self-esteem had been severely affected.

There are ways to help children with ADHD (Brown, Ilderton, Taylor, & Lock, 2001). One method is the medical model of giving them medication, usually a stimulant. Medicating children does not always solve the problem. There are children who need medication but do not get it, and other children who take medication but do not need it. There are also children who get medication, but the dose may not be appropriate. Teachers speak repeatedly of overmedicated children acting like "zombies."

When I first started doing research on ADHD, I became very concerned about the effects of stimulant medication on the developing brain. The preschool years are critical years for brain development. I believe it is every parent's responsibility to check this out thoroughly before beginning children on stimulant medication. On the other hand, I have to tell you a story about a man I met who spoke to me about medication. I will never forget him. I was in a small town in New Mexico. I had just completed a morning session for a large group of parents of children with ADHD. I was taking a break, and then I was going to do the same session for teachers. As I stood near my computer sorting through my PowerPoint presentation for the next session, a tall, slim, fair-haired man came up to me. He introduced himself to me as a dad whose son had been diagnosed the year before with ADHD. He told me that he had been very upset with the doctor when his son was placed on Ritalin because he did not want his son medicated. His ex-wife had custody, so it was her decision. But then something amazing happened; his son began to act totally different. He could focus. His grades dramatically improved. The dad was very impressed, and it made him start thinking about himself. He had had problems his whole life both in learning and in relationships. He decided to go to his son's doctor to see if he, too, had ADHD. The doctor did a full workup, diagnosed him with ADHD, and put him on Ritalin. This dad had a look of amazement on his face as he told me that up to the day he started taking Ritalin, he had never read a book from cover to cover. Once he started taking Ritalin, he got a library card and started reading book after book. He could focus. He could concentrate. I can still picture the look of awe on his face as he shared his story of how medication had helped him.

The American Psychiatric Association (2000) identifies several types of ADHD. All types have in common a chronic and persistent pattern of inattention, hyperactivity, and impulsivity.

ADHD INATTENTIVE TYPE

Children with this type of ADHD have many symptoms of being inattentive. One of the key symptoms is that they have trouble listening and following directions and have difficulty focusing and sustaining attention. They may start out listening to what the teacher is saying, but their minds drift off to other topics. This happens all the time, not only when in class. It can happen when children are playing in a learning center, building with blocks, "reading" a book, or listening to a friend. Their minds wander, and they are easily distracted. The distraction can be auditory like an airplane flying outside, raindrops on the window, or even air conditioning or heating vents. It can be visual like a fancy bulletin board at the front of the room or even something about the teacher's appearance.

Gardner was a preschooler with ADHD Inattentive Type. He was a quiet, shy boy, the type of child who could easily fall through the cracks. He did not misbehave or dress in any unusual way. His teacher, Mrs. Jenkins, was a first-year teacher. She put most of her attention on children who were misbehaving. One day, however, Mrs. Jenkins did notice Gardner. He was looking at her in a peculiar manner throughout circle time. She walked over to him and asked if something was wrong. He said, "Mrs. Jenkins, I was watching your hands—your red nail polish." He had become completely distracted by her nail polish. From that day on, Mrs. Jenkins never wore bright nail polish.

Because of this inattentiveness, children may start a task and not finish it. They are often inconsistent. Some days they may be able to focus better than others. On the days that they can't focus as well, they may look "spacey." Their attention just wanders from object to object and situation to situation. They may forget from moment to moment what they were doing.

Children with ADHD Inattentive Type have a tendency to procrastinate. They wait until the last possible minute to do something you have asked them to do. Waiting until the last minute actually stimulates the brain. When they feel rushed, they feel stimulated to focus and get the job done. It's their way of attending to a task. Of course, sometimes, the task doesn't get done at all because the child totally forgets about it. When they get into elementary school, this difficulty completing tasks generally affects their grades adversely (Reiter, 2004).

While children with ADHD generally have difficulty focusing, there are times when they can hyper-focus on something and tune out everything and everyone else. A great example of this is when children use the computer or watch television. Everything is tuned out for hours at a time.

When they are engaged in a project they love at preschool, this same hyper-focusing characteristic can help children stay focused on something for long periods of time.

Another characteristic of inattentive children is that they are often disorganized. They may lose or forget their belongings. These are the children who come to preschool without their "show and tell" objects on Show and Tell day. Their cubbies may be total disasters with objects scattered everywhere and items upside down. All of this contributes to these children feeling like "I can't get anything right. Why even try?" Once this type of learned helplessness occurs, it will be even harder to help children succeed (Valas, 2001). This child can be helped. It simply takes new tools. Figure 2.1 is a checklist of behavioral characteristics of ADHD Inattentive Type.

Figure 2.1 Checklist of Behavioral Characteristics of ADHD Inattentive Type

---

Checklist of Behavioral Characteristics of ADHD Inattentive Type

- ☐ Difficulty listening
- ☐ Difficulty attending to tasks
- ☐ Difficulty focusing
- ☐ Easily distracted
- ☐ Procrastinates
- ☐ Problems concentrating
- ☐ Inconsistent performance
- ☐ Disorganized
- ☐ Loses belongings
- ☐ Cluttered cubby and play area
- ☐ Forgetful
- ☐ Problems playing independently

Strategies for Succeeding With Children With ADHD Inattentive Type

The Edutainer

"Edutainer" is a word that I made up many years ago. An edutainer is both an educator and an entertainer. You have to do this to hold the attention of children. Be so engaging that children want to listen to you as much as they want to watch their favorite television show or play a video game. There was a time when children came to preschool, and even if they had ADHD, they sat still and listened as best as they could. They had that old-fashioned R-word: respect. They learned at home that when they came to preschool, they had better pay attention. That is generally not the case anymore. Instead, children come to preschool with an entirely different attitude: "Entertain me." They are used to watching television, playing video games, seeing entertainment. Now, as part of educating, teachers have to entertain, too. That is what it means to be an edutainer.

At seminars I show an awesome video clip that illustrates this point. A man is standing on a stage and starts to play his trombone. He hooks his audience's attention immediately by swinging his hips and rolling around on stage as he plays the trombone. He has zest; he has spirit. Soon, the audience members stand up and start swinging to the beat. He has captivated their attention. Everyone in my own audience laughs as they see this, and some get up and start swinging around just from watching it. He is an edutainer.

Brain research shows that there are different ways to engage the brain (Jenson, 2000). One fun way is to do something novel. For example, the first time I got on a plane after 9/11, I was feeling frightened. Usually, flight attendants give a tedious speech about seatbelts and oxygen masks right before the planes take off, and typically, passengers tune it out because they have heard it so many times before. This time, when many passengers were uneasy, the flight attendant greeted us all with a smile and instead of droning on, she sang the safety information. She deliberately made funny voice inflections as she sang. She was an edutainer and held our attention totally. This is a technique you can use. Laugh and have fun. Burst into song unexpectedly. Edutain and help all children focus and pay attention.

Eliminating Distractions

Because children with ADHD are so easily distracted, noise level and seating are crucial (Carroll et al., 2006). Noises can be extremely distracting.

If they sit near an air conditioning or heating vent, they may find it very difficult to concentrate on any activities because they are busy listening to the noise of the air from the vent. If they sit near the door, they can hear the sounds from the hallway. It's not only sounds that are distracting, but also sights. Children sitting near a window will be easily distracted by the sights outside the window. If children with ADHD are sitting near the back of the circle, all of the children in front of them will distract them. They will notice what the other children are wearing, what they are doing, and how they are sitting, instead of putting their attention on you.

Small Circles   Cut out circles about 6 to 8 inches in diameter from construction paper. Write on each circle the name of a child in your class. Have enough circles so that all children have their own circles. Next to each child's name, put a unique identifying sticker. Laminate each circle.

Before circle time, lay the circles out on the floor where you want each child to sit. It is always best to put the child who is easily distracted either next to an assistant if you have one, or right next to you.

Everything visible can make a difference. Some children are distracted by long earrings worn by teachers because they move around as the teacher speaks. Still other children are distracted by walls and nearby shelves with fun items on them. One morning I was observing a circle activity in an early childhood classroom. Little Josh had already been moved to sit beside the teacher because he was having a hard time sitting still. The problem was that his teacher was sitting on the floor right next to the bookshelves. I watched Josh stare at the books rather than at Miss Cathy, his teacher. He looked at the books and looked at the books, and then suddenly he reached out and took one of the books. As he did so, the entire bookshelf fell down in the middle of the circle! All of the children screamed with both fear and delight at this new development in their circle time.

Children with ADHD notice everything (Carroll et al., 2006). Their attention can be caught by sights and sounds you take for granted. If a child starts showing symptoms of inattentiveness, something as simple as changing the child's seat can totally change the child's behavior.

Headphones   Early childhood classrooms have a degree of noise as children play and talk. However, there are some children who are so distracted by the sounds that they cannot focus and may become irritable. They need something to block out the noise. Headphones or earplugs are a way of blocking out distractions. Keep them in a special place on a shelf and tell the children they can use them when the noise level is too loud.

Whisper Sign   Make a sign using poster board. Write the word "whisper" on the sign. Use a bright color for the sign like hot pink, or one that quickly catches the attention of all children. When the noise level gets loud, either you or another child can hold up the "whisper" sign until everyone in the classroom begins whispering. This will help keep the noise level down and prevent distractions. This is especially beneficial for children who are extremely sensitive to sounds.

Private Offices   An effective way to help young children stay attentive when they are working with materials that require their attention is to give them "private offices." Open two manila file folders side by side. Slide one of the folders partially into the other folder so that the folders overlap, creating three "walls." The "private office" can stand up on a table. Have children individualize the offices by decorating the outsides of the folders, but the insides remain blank. When children need to concentrate, they get out their "offices" and have privacy.

Staying on Task

Job Chart   It can be very difficult for children with ADHD to stay on task. There are several ways you can help them (Parker, 2005). One way is for you to use job charts. Have a list of jobs on a poster board. Take a photo of a child doing the task and place it next to each of the jobs. Assign children specific jobs each week by putting their photo and name next to the job. For example, have the words "empty trash" as one of the jobs. Next to the words, put a photo of a trashcan in your room. Every week, assign this job to a different child. Put the child's name and a photo of the child next to the picture of the trashcan. That way, the child knows what to do. Do this for all children. Visual reminders are a wonderful way to help children who are easily distracted and may forget what they are supposed to do.

Child's Name Card   Make name cards for children at the beginning of the school year. You can use large colored index cards or make your own out of construction paper. Write each child's name on the name cards. Next to each name, place the child's individualized sticker, the same one that you used for making the circle time "circles." Children will learn to identify the sticker as being unique to them. Laminate the name cards. Use the name cards as reminders for children of what to do next. For example, you may want a group of children to do a cooking project while other children are playing in centers. Have the children's names on name cards to determine whose turn it is to come next to the cooking project. When children find their name there, they know it is time to cook.

Proximity Control   Proximity control is an excellent method for helping all children, not just those with ADHD, stay on task (Gunter & Shores, 1995). When you see a child whose attention is wandering, who has that special glint in the eyes that says, "I'm getting ready to do something mischievous," walk over and stand or sit near the child. You don't have to say a word. Just your presence will almost always catch the child's attention and the child will become calmer and more focused. This is an effective strategy for nipping problems in the bud before they develop into classroom management issues.

Organizing Tools

One of the characteristics of children with ADHD Inattentive Type is disorganization. Look at the areas of disorganization and then focus on finding strategies to help children succeed, like color coding and labeling.

Color Coding   Color coding is an effective strategy to help children with ADHD stay organized (Brown et al., 2001). Use different colors for different learning centers. For example, the language learning center has little blue dots on the back of all of the materials. The shelves have blue dots. The science learning center has green dots, and the art center has yellow dots. When children remove something from the shelves, they look at the little dots on the materials and know exactly to which learning center they belong so they can easily put items back.

Pictures of Materials   Mrs. Bloom, an early childhood teacher, observed the dots and it gave her another idea. She took photos of all of the items on shelves and taped the photos to the shelves. Children always knew where items belonged on the shelves. They had their little dot to guide them to the right learning center and then they had the actual photo on the shelves so they could place the item where it belonged.

Label   Label everything. Have cubbies clearly labeled with children's names and their special stickers. Have a photo beside the cubby showing where everything needs to go. Have a set time each day for children to do a daily check to make sure everything is in the correct place.

Name Stickers on Work   It's a good idea to get children used to putting their names on their papers even though most preschoolers cannot write. The reason is that children with ADHD often forget to put their names on their papers when they are older. Give each child their special sticker. When children start a paper, they get their sticker and use it in a special place on the paper to symbolize their names. (Older children can also write their names next to the stickers.) You can help them remember to do this by highlighting papers ahead of time with yellow highlighter in the area on the page for the child's name. Have the children put their stickers or "write" their names where the yellow highlighter is marked on their sheets.

Another fun method for having children "write" their names is called "crayons in the air." When it is time for children to do something using paper, have them get out their sheets of paper and play a "Simon Says" type of game. They love games. They have to do everything that you tell them to do. Give them a bunch of silly instructions like, "Touch your nose," and then tell them, "Crayons in the air." The children all hold up their crayons. The next instruction is, "Crayons down on the top of the paper." This is followed by, "Write your names on the paper." Children attempt to write their names on their sheets of paper. After that, there are usually more fun instructions like having children smile at someone sitting next to them, putting their hands on top of their heads, clapping their hands, and even saying, "This is so much fun!" Children laugh and have fun doing this.

Peer Support

Assign children with ADHD who are forgetful a "remember partner." The remember partner is a child who is very organized and enjoys being a helper (Parker, 2005). The remember partner's job is to remind the child of important things to do. Choose the remember partner carefully because it is important that the two children are compatible.

Launching Pad

Children often forget to bring items to preschool. Suggest that parents create a "launching pad" area at home. It can be a chair or a small table. The children put a change of clothes, a sweater, a show and tell object, and anything else that needs to be brought to class on the launching pad.

ADHD HYPERACTIVE-IMPULSIVE TYPE

Just as the word *hyperactive* implies, children with this form of ADHD are very active and need to move around (Frank, 2001). They are often restless and cannot sit still for long periods of time. They are in constant motion. These are the children who roam around the room, and when sitting sometimes even fall out of their chairs. When they are sitting, they may be moving their hands, tapping their fingers, or swinging their legs back and forth. Their mouths are in motion too, talking, blurting out inappropriately, or chewing on a crayon or other object.

They are often frustrated, and may become angry with others and say things they do not mean. Sometimes, they don't even remember what it is they said that got someone upset. They just said what popped into their minds without thinking through the ramifications. This causes hurt feelings and sometimes failed relationships.

While it is easy to become upset with these children, it's important to remember that they do have a disorder. It is as real as diabetes. Underneath all the hyperactivity and impulsive behavior may be a very lonely child. Figure 2.2 is a checklist of behavioral characteristics of ADHD Hyperactive-Impulsive Type.

Figure 2.2 Checklist of Behavioral Characteristics of ADHD Hyperactive-Impulsive Type

---

Checklist of Behavioral Characteristics of ADHD Hyperactive-Impulsive Type

- ☐ High activity level
- ☐ Appears to be in constant motion
- ☐ Plays with objects
- ☐ Puts objects in mouth
- ☐ Talks excessively
- ☐ Difficulty waiting for turn
- ☐ Roams around classroom
- ☐ Great difficulty staying in seat
- ☐ Often fidgets with hands or feet
- ☐ Impulsive and lacks self-control
- ☐ Blurts out verbally
- ☐ Engages in impulsive behaviors
- ☐ Gets in trouble frequently
- ☐ Difficulty in personal relationships
- ☐ Often interrupts others
- ☐ Difficulty with transitions
- ☐ Easily frustrated

Strategies for Succeeding With Children With ADHD Hyperactive-Impulsive Type

The strategies you will be learning in this section are all designed to provide appropriate ways for children to move within the classroom. They need to move. It helps them concentrate and stay focused. It is not something that they *want* to do, but rather something that they *have* to do.

Mouse Pad

Children who are hyperactive often fidget with their hands. They often tap their fingers or objects loudly on tables. Give these children something else to tap—something that does not make noise. A computer mouse pad is perfect. When children feel like tapping their fingers or objects, they tap the mouse pad and no one is disturbed. Children get to tap, and the classroom gets to be quieter.

Kyle was in constant trouble for making too much noise in the classroom. He couldn't sit still; he was in constant motion. He continually tapped objects on tables. It was so loud that it distracted the entire class. When Kyle was 5 years old, everything changed for him. His teacher, Ms. Saven, taught him a new strategy. She told him it was OK with her if he tapped objects. She gave him a computer mouse pad and told him that anytime he felt like tapping, he was to tap the object on the mouse pad. He continued to tap, but now he was not disturbing anyone. He had learned an appropriate behavior to substitute for the inappropriate behavior. This method, along with others in this section, helped Kyle to thrive in his classroom. He had learned new behaviors to replace the old, inappropriate ones.

Energy Ball

You will need a stress ball for this strategy. Call it an "energy ball." Children take their excess energy and use it to squeeze the ball. They squeeze and squeeze the ball until they feel better and are able to keep their hands and bodies still. In one classroom that used this technique successfully, quiet, shy Megan came up to her teacher one day with a question. She said, "Miss Brook, if the other kids can put their energy into the ball, can I use it to get some energy? I'm really tired today because I couldn't fall asleep last night." Miss Brook said, "Sure," and Megan squeezed it and squeezed it until she felt better!

Stress Bucket

Some teachers have a "stress bucket" filled with different-shaped stress balls. They add to the bucket cut-up squares of soft fabric like velvet and even small squares of cut-up shag carpeting. This is effective because children like to squeeze different textures.

Velcro

There are some children who may become embarrassed when classmates see them holding a stress object in their hands. Place a small square of Velcro under a special table. Show children where it is and tell them that when they feel like moving their hands, they can rub the Velcro.

Doodle Pad

Take a tablet of paper and call it a "doodle pad." When children feel like moving, they get a sheet of the paper and "doodle" all over it until they feel better and are able to sit still.

Twist Bracelets

Some children who move their hands excessively develop a habit of twisting and pulling on their hair, and they actually can pull their hair out from their scalp. Teach them a different strategy for their hands when they feel like twisting something by giving them a small rope bracelet. Whenever they feel like twisting their hair, they twist the bracelet instead. Be careful that children do not twist the bracelet so strongly that they harm their wrists. If you see this happening, suggest that they hold and twist the bracelet rather than wear it.

Errands

It's readily apparent which children need to move their entire bodies. They fidget and sometimes even fall out of their seats. They need strategies that will allow them to move their legs without disrupting the class. One effective strategy is to give these children errands within the classroom. They can empty the trash, help clean shelves, or carry something from one end of the room to the other.

Empty Desk

When you have children who need to move their entire bodies, use the empty desk strategy. Have an empty desk or small table. When children need to move, they move quietly to the other desk without touching anyone or talking. There are some children who go back and forth between the two desks every 10–15 minutes. As long as children do it quietly without disrupting the class, this is allowable.

Jog Laps

Some children need to move so much that they run around the classroom. Some actually run outside of the classroom. I know teachers who have had to chase them, and sometimes the children are faster than their teacher! Here is an effective strategy. Get some colored masking tape and mark a large circle or oval area in the room on the floor with the tape. Be careful to put it somewhere there is no clutter and no danger of children falling. Have children who are "runners" bring a special pair of "jogging shoes" to the center. When children feel like running, they put on their jogging shoes (a pair of sneakers) and jog around the circle and count the laps. When they feel better and are able to sit still, they stop and remove their jogging shoes, put on their regular shoes, and go back to doing whatever the class is doing.

BOTH ADHD INATTENTIVE AND ADHD HYPERACTIVE-IMPULSIVE TYPES

Strategies for Succeeding With Children With ADHD Inattentive Type and Children With ADHD Hyperactive-Impulsive Type

Time Frames

Children with ADHD generally have no innate concept of time. They only see *now*, not the future and not the past. They generally tend to overestimate or underestimate how long it will take to complete specific tasks. They are task oriented rather than time structured. If interested in a task, children start it and work on it until it is finished or until they have collapsed from exhaustion. However, if the task is not interesting, children will typically avoid beginning the task at all.

The key is to make each task interesting and relevant. Make tasks come alive so that children are excited. The more relevant it is, the more they will want to do it.

Self-Monitoring

Children need to learn how to work independently. Teach them self-monitoring skills (Harris, Friedlander, Saddler, Frizzelle, & Graham, 2005). A stopwatch or timer is an effective way to help children self-monitor. Have a timer for children. Children stay in a learning center until the timer goes off. When it goes off, they put all their things away and go to the next center.

Clear Directions

Children with ADHD often do not follow directions because they do not fully understand them. The good news is that there are ways to give them directions so that they do understand (Frank, 2001). Give only one direction at a time, and demonstrate what you want them to do. Preschoolers need that visual explanation. Once you have demonstrated, have them take a turn rehearsing the directions. Keep directions brief. Use words that are easy for them to understand. Here's an example of clear directions about hand washing. This is something very important for young children because germs can spread so easily in child care programs.

Start by having all the materials ready. In this case, the lesson is at the sink. There is liquid soap in a pump bottle, paper towels, and the sink. These are the words I have said when teaching this lesson. Feel free to modify them to fit your own personal style. Keep the directions clear and visual.

"My children, I have something really important I want to teach you today. It's about how to wash your hands. Sometimes, if we don't wash our hands carefully, we can pass germs—little things on your hands that are invisible, but that can make other children and even yourself sick. So it's really important to wash your hands in a special way." (Pause while children talk about other children who have become sick at times.) "The first step in washing your hands is to turn the water on like this." (Turn the water on very slowly and deliberately. Make sure it is not coming out full force so that children splash water everywhere. Turn it on so it is a gentle but full stream of water.)

"This is the soap container. Hold it in one hand and put your other hand under this part—the pump. Now squeeze just one time and catch the soap with your other hand. Put the soap container down.

"Rub the soap into your hands and use a little water. Make a bunch of bubbles—lather. Keep washing up and down while you silently sing to yourself, 'Happy birthday to me, happy birthday to me, happy birthday dear me, happy birthday to me.'

"When you are finished singing, your hands will be ready to be rinsed off. Rinse off every little bit of soap." (Demonstrate as you tell them this.) "Now, it's time to shake your hands out over the sink." (Shake your hands out.) "Take one paper towel from the stack." (Take just one towel.) "Wipe your hands so they are no longer wet." (Demonstrate.) "Take the paper towel and toss it in the trashcan next to the sink." (Demonstrate.)

"Now, it's your turn to help me. What should I do first?" Go through the whole process again with them telling you what to do. Then have one of the children take a turn. Choose a child who always gets it right to demonstrate.

Traffic Light Signals

Most children are embarrassed to say that they do not understand something being taught or cannot figure out how to do a task. To constantly monitor whether your class understands, make several traffic light signals for the children. Take a white sheet of paper and fold it vertically into three equal sections. On each section, draw a huge circle. Fill in the circle on the top section with green to make the "green light." Fill in the middle circle with yellow for the "yellow light." Fill in the bottom circle with red to be the "red light." Fold the paper back into three equal parts so it can stand up with one side facing the front of the classroom. Pass out the traffic light signals to your children to keep in their cubbies. Explain that when they understand something, they can get out their traffic light signal and have it on "green" facing the front of the room. When they are not quite sure, they set the traffic light on "yellow" to face the front of the classroom. When they have no idea what they are supposed to be doing or learning, they have the "red light" face the front of the classroom. It's an effective way of continually assessing children so you know who needs your help.

Sometimes children playing together in a learning center need help. They can go to their cubbies to get their traffic light signals. For example, Sammy, Jonas, and Krist were all playing together trying to build a space shuttle in the block center. Everything kept falling down over and over again and they were getting very frustrated. Jonas said, "I'm going to go get the red light so Ms. Simpson can see we need help." That is exactly what he did. When Ms. Simpson was circulating through the room and saw the "red" traffic light signal, she stopped to help the boys.

Frequent Support and Encouragement

Your smile is worth riches to children who struggle. Affirm children when they act appropriately (Bowman, Carr, Cooper, Miles, & Toner, 1998). Let them know that you believe in them. Your positive words and comments can make a huge difference in the lives of your children. You just never know the difference you make. Kasinda was a really tough child I had in my early childhood classroom. She was taller than any other child in my class, very slim, with a long, dark ponytail and huge, hardened eyes. She had a hard time concentrating. She would start to do something, and then forget what she was going to do and retreat into her own world. She was angry often, talked back when asked to do anything, and treated me and all the other children with disrespect. I checked into her background and learned that her dad had left before she was born, and her mom had left a few years later. She was being raised by an elderly grandmother who was exhausted. The grandmother felt like a failure because of what had happened with her daughter and now had just given up on Kasinda.

I resolved that I would help Kasinda. I set aside a special time each day to meet with her alone for five minutes. I told her that I wanted to get to know her and mostly listened as she talked. The early sessions were frequently for her to vent anger. She told me she hated her mommy and her daddy and even her grandmother. Slowly, she began to trust me. She had no friends. Actually, children avoided her. I asked her if she would like to have friends, and she thought about that for nearly a week, and then one day she said, "Yes." I paired her up with a "class pal." Soon she and her "class pal" became friends. It was amazing to watch Kasinda blossom. I continued to set aside special time with her every day. Her eyes became brighter, and she went from an unhappy, sullen child to a much happier child. What a joy!

One day, many years later, I was leading a seminar, and a tall, attractive woman came up to me and introduced herself. It was Kasinda! She had on her great smile. She was now a teacher and loved her work. She thanked me for taking the time to be there for her when she really needed it and she said that she became a teacher so she could do the same thing for other children. You just never know the difference that you make each day in the lives of your children.

How to Handle   **3**
Children With
Learning
Disabilities

Today's child is tomorrow's future.

—Maryln Appelbaum

This topic has very special meaning for me because two close family members were both labeled with learning disabilities (LD). They are both adults now, and while they had many struggles they had to overcome as children, they are now both successful in their lives. I share this story at the beginning of this chapter because, even though having LD can be devastating, there is hope.

Individuals with LD have a neurological impairment that mixes up signals between the brain and the senses (Winebrenner, 2006). Children with LD may have an average or above-average intelligence. They can see and hear, but they do it differently. They have a neurological impairment in perception, conceptualization, language, memory, attention, or motor control. LD affects approximately 5 percent of children (American Psychiatric Association, 2000).

Here is an exercise that I use at the beginning of every seminar I teach about LD. I have audience members pair up and say the alphabet backwards. Then I have them do it again, but with a twist. They have to say the alphabet backwards, and between each letter they must insert the name of a city, country, or state that does not begin with those two letters (e.g., "Z, California, Y").

Audience members all flounder, grin sheepishly, and say that this task is very difficult. I then explain that this is how learning feels for children with LD. Learning something new is this difficult and frustrating for children with LD.

Children hear the sounds, but their brains may mix up the signals. The same is true for what they see. Here is an example of how differently children with LD can see. Imagine that your preschoolers with LD can read, and you have up on the board the sentence, "The train goes fast." It may look to children with LD like, "The rain goes fast." They may omit just one letter, totally changing the context. They may omit an entire word, and the sentence could read, "The goes fast." Words may be blurred so that they are hard to read. Every time they read the same sentence or word, it can change again. If you think that sounds frustrating for you, just imagine how frustrating that is for children with LD.

Children with LD may also have problems with long-term memory. They may struggle to learn a concept and then later forget it. It is erased to the point that it does not seem like it was ever learned. If all of this appears frustrating to teachers, it is even more frustrating for children. Children struggle with feeling like they are dumb, even though they may actually be bright. As they get older, they often suffer from low self-esteem because of feeling like failures in school. Nearly 40 percent of children with LD drop out of school (American Psychiatric Association, 2000). They need strategies to help them feel successful and people to believe in them.

It is rare that a child in your early childhood program will already have been diagnosed with LD. Generally they are not diagnosed until they have been in elementary school, and even then, it may not occur until third or fourth grade (Appelbaum, 2008). However, there are signs that you may see in your preschoolers. Figure 3.1 lists common symptoms of LD in young children.

If you suspect a child has a learning difference, it is important that there is early diagnosis so that the child can begin getting help in addition to the strategies you can provide in the classroom.

STRATEGIES FOR SUCCEEDING WITH CHILDREN WITH LD

You can help children with LD. The first step is to recognize that these children are not lazy or unmotivated. They have a real disability. They may become unmotivated if they continue to fail. Your task is to help keep them motivated by finding strategies that work.

Figure 3.1 Symptoms of LD in Young Children

Symptoms of LD in Young Children
• Delay in expressive language
• Problems comprehending verbal language
• Difficulty following directions
• Lack of interest in print materials like books
• Problems or delays with fine and gross motor skills
• Problems with writing
• Inattentive
• Easily distracted
• Difficulty with transitions
• Delays in emergent literacy skills
• Letter reversals
• Problems remembering new words
• Forgetfulness of concepts previously learned

SOURCE: National Joint Committee on Learning Disabilities (2007).

Strategies for ADHD

Many of the strategies suggested in the previous chapter apply to children with LD. They, too, benefit from all of the organizational strategies as well as other strategies. Review the strategies for ADHD and use them with your children who have LD.

General Strategies

Individualize Instruction

Children are not in a "one-size-fits-all" category. Every child is different. Every child learns differently. It is important to individualize instruction. When you do something, and it does not work, do something else. Build a program on children's individual strengths and needs, and it will be successful (National Joint Committee on Learning Disabilities, 2007).

I can still remember my first years teaching when I tried to teach all the children at the same time in the same way. They were frustrated, and so was I. It did not work. I had lots of classroom management problems. When I individualized instruction, I had an inclusive classroom with all children working at their own ability levels.

Literacy Strategies

Because reading is often a real problem for children with LD, it is important to have a bag of tricks to help children succeed.

Print-Rich Environment

All children benefit from a print-rich environment. Children with LD benefit even more. They become accustomed to print everywhere. Label, label, and label some more. Label cubbies with the word "Cubby." Label the tables with the words "Art Table," "Food Table," etc. Label the shelves. Have little labels on shelves by materials. For example, on the language shelves have words in front of the objects such as "Pencils," "Crayons," "Paper, "Chalkboard," and "Chalk."

Book Nook

Have a cozy book nook. It needs to be a warm and safe place so children want to go there and look at the books. You may add some pillows or a rocking chair. Have a bookshelf with age-appropriate books. All children enjoy picture books.

Story Time

Have regularly scheduled story times. Choose books that have fun stories for children. Make the stories enjoyable. I visited one classroom where the teacher was surrounded by children as she prepared to read a story. I saw two 3-year-olds who looked really mischievous, and I wondered how she would handle them. She captivated all the children, including those two boys, immediately with her opening statements. She said, "I have a really exciting story I am going to read you today, and it has a huge surprise in it. It is something that will amaze you." She was very dramatic. She then started telling the children the story. She painted a word picture so that children could "see in their minds" what she was saying. When she saw that she might lose the children, she said very dramatically, "I wonder if the surprise is on the next page. . . . Let's see." The children acted like they were hypnotized. They were all sitting, waiting for the "surprise." My guess is that this teacher does something special for children every time she reads. The more children enjoy stories, the more they will enjoy picking up books and becoming familiar with print.

Child Authors

I go into a lot of preschools to observe and to make video clips for seminars. I have seen some amazing homemade books in book nooks. One book I recently saw was called "About Our Class." The teacher asked the children to each draw what they liked best about the class. Afterward, the teacher asked each child to describe what they drew. They dictated as she wrote what they said on their artwork. All of the pages were then put together to make a book for the book nook.

That is just one example. I have seen books called "Our Favorite Pets" and "Our Favorite Foods." The theme of favorites can be expanded to many areas in the classroom, even favorite books and favorite activities. Still another creative book is the "Book of Kindness." Children do kind acts for other children or at home. Those acts of kindness are then drawn by the children, and a little note is added by the teacher. This is a great way to not only encourage a love for literacy to help children with LD and other children, but a wonderful way to teach them to do acts of kindness for others.

Story Boxes

This is another great way to make literacy come alive. Find a book that you and the children will enjoy. Read the story to yourself. Find all the objects to make the story come alive. For example, if you were reading Goldilocks and the Three Bears, you would have in a box a momma bear, a daddy bear, and a baby bear. You would also have objects or photos of objects like three beds. Tell the story to the children and as you read, get out the corresponding objects. When the story is finished, carefully put the objects back into the box. Tell the children they too can practice "reading" the story and taking out the objects. They love it. It's adorable to watch them pretending to read the book and maneuvering the objects. This instills confidence in literacy skills—confidence that they will need to get them through tougher times.

Colored Transparencies

When children actually begin reading, a simple correction that helps many of them read better is placing colored transparent sheets of paper over their reading material. Suddenly, words that were blurred and jumbled on white paper become clearer and easier to read. Different children need different colors of transparent sheets. Inexpensive sheets are often available at a scrapbooking store, and you can purchase a variety of colors to determine which colors work best for the children.

Show the different colors to children with LD who have problems reading. Place them on top of pages of white paper with black print. Ask the children to tell you which colors work best. Many children choose yellow, but other children may choose another color. Once you know the color that helps the child, you can recommend that parents buy glasses with lenses in that color. Transparent sheets may become blurry with hand and fingerprints. Lenses in the glasses can be more easily cleaned.

Recorded Books

Children listen to recorded books while looking at the pictures as they "read" the actual book. This is especially good for auditory learners. Discover the way each of your children learns best, and you will have gone a long way to helping them succeed.

Phonological Awareness and Phonemic Awareness

Phonological awareness is the awareness of the spoken language in all its forms, words, sentences, phrases, and phonemes (Kemp & Eaton, 2008). Phonemes are one component of phonological awareness, but separate because without the ability to understand the individual words, there can be no comprehension of phrases and sentences. Phonemic awareness is a subset of phonological awareness, and it is an important bridge to learning to read (Woods, 2003). It is the ability to identify and use individual units of sounds—phonemes. For example, the word "mat" has three individual sounds, "m," "a," and "t." This is an area of weakness for many children with LD. The more they practice, the better they generally can perform.

Sandpaper Letters

Children trace a sandpaper letter with their fingers and as they trace the letter, they say the sound over and over again. For example, for the letter "m," the children say, "mmmmmmmm," "mmmmmmmm." The children learn three sounds at a time. It is easier for children to begin with consonants. If you do not have sandpaper letters, simply draw a large letter, and have the children trace it over and over again saying the sound as they trace it.

Matching Sounds and Objects

Have a small basket that has in it objects that begin with two consonants the children have learned. Have the consonants on two small cards. Children put the objects that begin with the consonants underneath the corresponding letters. For example, under the "m" could be the following tiny plastic objects: mouse, money, mat, man. Under the "b" could be the following tiny objects: ball, bat, bone, banjo. You can do this same exercise having children match the sounds to picture cards rather than objects.

Once the objects are lined up under the letter cards, have children "read" the columns they have made: "mmmm," "mmmmouse," "mmmmoney," "mmmmat," "mmmman." They do the same with the objects that begin with "b." It is self-correcting because they can hear the sounds and correct themselves when they make a mistake.

Finding Beginning Sounds

Teach children to look for things or people in the classroom that begin with the sounds they have learned. They may point to a child named "Brittany" for the "b" sound. They see a tiny bell on a shelf and point it out for the "b" sound.

Lining Up to Sounds

This is a fun game that children enjoy. Say, "Everyone whose name begins with 'b' line up at the door now." Once those children have lined up, do the same with other letters until all the children have lined up at the door. In the beginning, you will have to help them to identify the first letter in their names.

Identifying Phonemes (Individual Sounds)

Tell the children two words that have a common phoneme. Have the children tell you what the sound is that both words have in common. For example, it can be "ball" and "basket." The common sound they will say is "b." It could even be an ending sound. For example, "mat" and "bat," and the common ending sound is "t."

Rhyming Skills

Children enjoy fun rhyming activities. They are a good way to help develop reading readiness (Woods, 2003). Teach them poems and songs that rhyme. Ask them to tell you all the words that rhyme with "mat," such as "bat," "hat," "cat," "fat," "sat." Tell them four words and ask them which one does not rhyme, such as "bat," "cat," "house," "sat."

Playing Word Games

Word games help children manipulate words and sounds (Woods, 2003). Have the children tell you two words they hear in the word "raincoat." What two words do they hear in "hot dog"? Children love games like this.

Tactfulness

Be tactful. When children make an error involving literacy, instead of immediately correcting them, offer corrections in a more positive manner. Instead of saying, "That's wrong, Jeff," say, "Let me show you another way to do this." These are children who easily feel like failures. The more they feel like they cannot succeed, the more they really cannot succeed. Your words can help ease the discomfort of making a mistake. Your voice tone is as important as your words. When they hear, "I believe in you—you can do this," in your voice, it helps them to believe in themselves, too.

Fun and Interesting Books

Have you ever read a book that you just could not put down? You read and read and read, putting off doing other things. The book had you totally hooked. Finding a fascinating book is important for children with LD. Find out what interests them, and offer them books and articles to read in their area of interest.

Michael was a 5-year-old that I suspected might have LD. He hated books. He struggled with anything involving literacy and avoided the book nook and all reading and writing activities. I discovered that he was interested in fish. He had a fish tank at home and knew the names of and interesting details about each of the fish. I brought him a book filled with pictures of fish, and he liked it so much that he wanted me to read it to him over and over again. He often went into the book nook to look at the book himself and "pretend read." I used that book as a jump-start to get him engaged in other themes the class was studying. When we were learning about Alaska, I gave him a book about the different types of fish that were native to Alaska. You can use this strategy with your children; find their hooks, their subjects of interest, and build on them.

Story boxes are a fun way to make books come to life. All you need is a shoebox, a storybook that the children love, and a few props that are part of the story. As the children turn the pages in the book, they pull out the props and act out the story. This is a great activity for individual children and for small groups of children. For example, at one preschool I saw the book *Mrs. Wishy Washy*, by Joy Cowley, along with a small bowl for a tub, a tiny cow, duck, pig, and a little doll that represented the character of Mrs. Wishy Washy. All of these items were in a shoebox. The children had lots of fun with this story box. Find your own books that children love to read and create story boxes for them.

Writing

Children with LD often have trouble writing. They may make reversals and have difficulty making and forming letters.

Provide a Model

Children often reverse letters or numerals. One effective strategy is to have a model for them. Write letters on a piece of paper. Have arrows showing where to start. Children trace the letters over and over again until it became second nature to write the letters correctly.

Hidden Answers

There may be another reason for the reversals. I had a child in my school named Cory. He was a good-natured, short, and chubby kindergartner. Cory's dad was the president of a large bank and was used to telling people what to do and how to do it. He was frustrated with Cory's reversals, especially with the letters "b" and "d." I met with Cory's father at a teacher conference. He told me he had practiced and practiced with Cory, but Cory still kept making reversals. He said that Cory used to write with his left hand and that it took him months to get Cory to use his right hand. He was pleased that Cory was finally using his right hand after months of nagging.

The next day, I decided to do an experiment with Cory. I gave him a sheet of paper and told him to write some words that had the letters "b" and "d" sprinkled throughout. I told him that this time, I wanted him to write with his left hand. At first, he did not want to use his left hand. He told me that his dad told him not to use it. Finally, he agreed for that one time to use his left hand. Cory copied the words perfectly with no reversals at all. I called his dad and told him what happened, and he agreed that from that time on, Cory could use his left hand. Cory never had any further problems with reversals.

Prepare the Hand

One of the most important strategies for teaching children to write is to prepare the hand. Look at your hand right now as you are reading this. Pretend to hold a pencil. You are holding together your thumb, forefinger, and middle finger. Those are called "pincer fingers," which are the fingers that grip a pencil or pen. The more you prepare children to use those fingers, the better they will be able to write.

An excellent exercise for the pincer fingers is "tonging." You will need two same-sized small soup bowls, a pair of tongs, a sponge cut into small pieces, and a tray that holds all of the items. Fill the bowl on the left with the cut-up pieces of sponge. The bowl on the right is empty. Demonstrate slowly taking the tongs and moving one sponge at a time from the left bowl to the right bowl. When you are finished, turn the tray so that the full bowl is once again on the left. Make sure children always use the tongs from left to right, because you are indirectly training their eyes to go from left to right. That is the way children read a book and write—from left to right.

Once children have mastered tonging using large tongs, replace the tongs with tweezers and smaller objects. Children use the tweezers to move smaller objects from the bowl on the left to a bowl on the right.

The more those pincer fingers are developed, the better children will be able to write. It is similar to developing muscles when going to a gym. Several years ago, my son and daughter-in-law bought me a gym membership for my birthday. When I went to the gym, the trainers started me with very small weights. Gradually, over time, they gave me larger and larger weights. First, I had to learn how to handle the weights, how to hold them, and how to lift them. It is the same with teaching writing. The hand needs to be prepared before children can lift those pencils or pens and begin writing.

Tracing

When children are ready to start writing, have them trace the letter with their fingers. Have them practice making letters on a chalkboard, where the letters can be easily erased. When they have mastered the chalkboard, they are ready to write their letters on a sheet of paper.

Math Strategies

Math is a subject that children with LD may find a struggle. It is important to help children feel successful so that they develop self-confidence.

Making Math Concrete

Learning math involves taking an abstract concept and making it concrete in the minds of children. The best way to teach math is to use manipulatives that children can see, feel, and count. They need to be able to see what different numbers look like. That is why so many children count on their fingers. Those children are actually saying to you, "I learn best when I see, feel, and touch the numbers." The more concretely you teach math, the more easily children will learn.

Counting as a Foundation

You can learn to read without memorizing the alphabet, but it is impossible to do any math operations without knowing how to count. Children need to learn one-to-one correspondence. They have to learn that what they are saying corresponds to objects. Ask them to hand you one of an object. Have them take two objects and place them somewhere in the room. Count aloud whenever possible in your classroom. Count children as they line up. Count desks in the room. Count the days of the week. Count the hands of how many children have pets at home. Have children join you as you count. The more they count, the better prepared they will be for mathematical operations.

Whole Body Math

Another way to teach children to count is to have them stand up and move. Have them all stand up in a circle. Have them take "one" step inside the circle. Then have them take "two" steps "outside" of the circle. They are able to experience with their entire bodies what the numbers mean. It is another way of taking the abstract quality of math and making it concrete. Extend this to having them stand in a straight line and take three steps forward, one step backward, and two steps forward. Keep going. They love movement, and this is a great way for them to experience counting. The more multisensory experiences you use, the better the children can learn (Winebrenner, 2006).

A CONCLUDING STORY

Many years ago I had a college professor who told us a story about his graduating class. He said that he was part of a large graduating class, but the person who got the highest grades in his class was a student with LD.

That student had more of one ingredient than all the other students did. He did not have the highest IQ, the most financial wealth, or the best looks. He had something better than all the others, and it was motivation. That motivation kept him searching to find ways to succeed and to graduate at the top of his class. You, too, can do this for your children. You can give them the motivation that they need to succeed. Believe in them. See something that they do not yet see. And after a while, they will see it, too!

How to Handle Anger and Oppositional Defiant Disorder

Anger is one letter away from danger.

—Maryln Appelbaum

W hen I am speaking to audiences, early childhood teachers across the country, describe children as being more angry and aggressive than ever before. They tell me that children kick, hit, and throw things. One teacher described how one of the children in her class had on pointy cowboy boots and started kicking her. Still another teacher told me that one of the preschoolers tried to strangle another smaller child. This violence that begins so young later extends to older children. There was one time that I had to do an inservice training for an elementary school. There had been a shooting that resulted in the death of a student the day before I arrived. The teachers and administrators were all visibly frightened. I was frightened too and wondered if it would happen again while I was there. Sometimes, I have gone to schools where I have had to go through airport-like security just to enter the building. The world has changed, and there are more angry children now (Overstreet, 2000). The early years are a good time to nip this trend.

Angry children can and often do create chaos. They create crises everywhere—in halls, classrooms, and playgrounds. Situations can easily escalate and become out of control. Children seem to have more access to weapons and sometimes bring weapons to school. One teacher told me that a child brought a pocketknife for "Show and Tell." Other children become frightened and try to avoid angry, defiant children. Staff members who do not even know the angry children may have heard about them and also adopt a fearful attitude and avoid angry children. They, too, become angry—angry at the children with anger issues and angry with themselves for not being able to stand up to them. Still other children enjoy watching children become angry, and they set them up so they can see the anger emerge.

Is anger really a bad thing? The truth is that everyone reading these words has at some time in their lives been angry. Anger is a normal emotion. However, when it is expressed inappropriately, it becomes a problem.

Anger is a secondary emotion. It occurs after feeling one of the primary emotions—fear, frustration, powerlessness, worthlessness, unfairness, hurt, or loss. The primary emotion occurs first. Here is a true story that clearly illustrates this point. This happened many, many years ago. My daughter, Tobi, went on her first date. She was 16 years old. The boy came and picked her up. I gave her a curfew of 11:30 p.m. All evening I kept thinking about her and wondering how it was going. I was relieved when it was 11:00 p.m. because she would soon be home. Soon it was 11:30 and Tobi was not home. Then it was midnight, and she was still not home. This was the time before cell phones, so I couldn't call her to find out what was happening. By 12:30 a.m., I was in a total panic. At 1:00, I started calling hospitals to see if she had been admitted. At 1:15, she came home along with her date. I took one look at her and angrily said, "Where have you been? How could you stay out this late? Don't you know how worried I have been? You are in big, big trouble!"

This is a classic case of anger being a secondary emotion. My primary emotion had been fear. The secondary emotion was anger, and that is what Tobi experienced when she walked in the door. Fortunately, I quickly calmed down and listened. She took me outside and I saw a different car than the one she had gone out in. Inside the car were her date and his parents. His car had broken down, and he had only one quarter left after taking her for dinner. He used it to call his parents, and they came and picked them up. It would have been much better had I expressed my primary emotion when Tobi walked in and said, "I was so worried about you." I am older now and wiser, but children are not. They just express what they feel at the moment.

When children are angry, it's important to always think about what the primary emotion may have been. Was the child feeling frustrated about not being able to do a task? Did the child feel rejected by peers? In some cases, the primary emotion may not have happened at preschool but at home. The child may have displaced anger (Denson, Pedersen, & Miller, 2006). Displaced anger is anger that is felt toward another person or circumstance.

Benjie was a child with displaced anger. Benjie is now a young adult. He told me that as a child, he remembers feeling very frightened every time his mother got sick. She was frequently hospitalized with life-threatening illnesses starting when Benjie was 2 years old. Benjie couldn't show that he was afraid at home because he didn't want to make his mother feel worse in any way. Each time his mother went into the hospital, he acted out. He was angry and got in trouble. His feelings of fear and powerlessness translated into anger at school. No one connected with him to find out what was happening at home. The situation continued until secondary school, when one of his counselors realized what was happening. They talked, and she taught him new and more appropriate ways to handle his primary feelings.

Displaced anger also occurs in children who are being abused at home. They are terrified of the abuser and cannot say or do anything at home. Some of the children internalize the anger and become depressed. Others come to school with displaced anger and let it out on others.

Your goal is not to stifle the anger that young children have but, instead, to help them express it in a healthy way—a way that helps them express the primary emotion too. There are positive benefits of anger expressed appropriately. It provides a sense of release for children. It also clears the air so that others understand what is going on.

Not all children have displaced anger. Some children express anger because they are copying family members. Children grow up watching how their role models express anger. They see them yell and shout and even hit something. If children see adults rage and berate others when angry, that is what they learn as the appropriate way to express anger. They don't know any other way, so they do what they have seen, even if they didn't like it and even if they were themselves the victims of the anger.

In addition to family role models expressing anger, children also see role models in the media expressing anger (Anderson & Bushman, 2001). Children watch more television today than ever before. They see acts of violence in television programs on a daily basis. They see actors and actresses showing sarcasm and little respect when speaking to each other. They see people being killed and maimed as a way of getting retaliation and revenge. The news is filled with stories of violence. Children rarely see programs that teach restraint and problem solving in a peaceful way. They also play video games filled with violence. While children are playing those games, they routinely "kill" or erase people. That is how they win the game—by making others disappear.

Today's young children are more stressed than ever before, and this is a contributing factor to anger in children (Bagdi & Pfister, 2006). They are frequently rushed from one activity to another. They have very little opportunity to "blow off steam" with spontaneous play in their homes and neighborhoods. Instead, they often rush from their child care centers to shop with their parents for dinner, and even to lessons in skating and ballet. When they are home, they are often glued to their television sets watching violence and negativity. Stressed children can, and do, lose their tempers more frequently.

Suppressing anger can cause psychological difficulties. Children become like cans of soda pop that have been shaken over and over again. Eventually, that soda pop can explodes. The seal pops off, and there is soda pop everywhere. It's the same with children who have been bottling up anger. It bursts forth in many ways. The child may burst forth as a bully and hurt others. The child may become depressed from holding the anger inside. The child may start building a false world to escape from the real world. These effects of anger are all things that you need to prevent in children. The goal is to help children express themselves in positive and appropriate ways.

THE STAGES OF ANGER AND STRATEGIES FOR EACH STAGE

Stage 1: The Trigger Stage

Anger does not usually just flare up. There are four distinct stages that I have observed while teaching. I call them the Trigger Stage, the Turning Point Stage, the Firing Stage, and the Fall-Out Stage. Each stage calls for different strategies.

The first stage is the Trigger Stage. This is the stage in which children begin to become upset. They feel some type of primary emotion triggered by something upsetting. Children become upset, anxious, moody, and confused and may not be able to think clearly. This is the easiest stage to help children.

Greet and Read

Stand at the door and greet young children as they enter the classroom. I did this when I was teaching. I smiled and said welcoming words. As I spoke to them, I "read" their moods. I checked to see if they looked happy, sad, angry, or worried.

When you greet and read children, you know what approach to take with individual children. Mrs. Jenkins had attended one of my seminars and had learned to greet and read. One day, Mrs. Jenkins was standing at the door to greet and read children. She noticed that one child, Tory, looked upset. Tory was 4 years old and a happy, good-natured child. On this particular day, Tory looked different. He wasn't smiling. Mrs. Jenkins made a mental note to talk to Tory as soon as she had the other children busy with activities. A short time later, Mrs. Jenkins asked Tory if he was all right. Tory said that his parents had told him the night before that they were moving to another city. He was scared. He would miss his friends and her. He didn't want to start all over again. Tory talked while Mrs. Jenkins listened until Tory felt better. He had been bottling his feelings up inside, and the more he talked, the better he felt. It all started with Mrs. Jenkins greeting and reading Tory.

Mood Sticks

Some children are harder to read. Mood sticks are an excellent way to detect if something is wrong. This strategy takes a little preparation, but it is well worth the time. You will need four small empty baby food jars or similar-sized containers. You will also need craft sticks or tongue depressors and large stick-on labels. Make a label for each jar. Mark them "Happy," "Mad," "Sad," and "Worried." Draw a little face to match the word on each label so that children can "read" the label. Now, you are ready to involve the children. Hand out the craft sticks so that children each get their own craft stick. Have them individualize the sticks with their own individual art design. Write their names on the sticks. Place all the labeled craft sticks into a larger jar so that names are sticking out where children can see them.

When children enter the classroom, have them find their individualized craft sticks and place them into one of the mood jars describing their mood that day. You will immediately know the moods of your children so you can help them.

This strategy also has a bonus purpose. It is an easy method for taking attendance. The craft sticks left over in the larger bin are there because children are absent.

Moods Are Contagious

This Trigger Stage is very important. It's the earliest stage in which you can nip problems before they escalate into full-fledged anger. Your job during this phase is to help children stay coherent. Do this by being patient and calm. Use a calm, soothing voice when speaking to children. Your mood is contagious. If they hear in your voice that you are upset, there is a greater likelihood that they will become more upset. This is not the time to insist on rapid compliance on low-priority issues. Power struggles magnify and intensify anger.

Caution With Transitions

Some children have a tougher time with change, including the changes that can happen in classrooms. Throughout the day there are many transitions. One of the ways to minimize the impact of transitions is to have a schedule—a routine that is consistent. Children always know when the next event will happen. Warn all children ahead of time when there will be change. "In five minutes, it will be time to put everything away and line up to go outside." Just saying these simple words can prevent children from becoming stressed and anxious at a sudden change and minimize angry outbursts.

Music

Music is a calming influence on the classroom (Hallam, Price, & Katsarou, 2002) and can be used to prevent problems from occurring. Play calming music as children enter the classroom. Play special songs when there are transitions. If the entire class is starting to get "antsy," put some music on, and the mood in the classroom can change within seconds.

Anger Rules

Have rules about expressing anger. For example, one rule can be: "It's OK to be angry, but it's not OK to hurt another child, property, yourself, or the teacher." This can prevent problems before they happen. Discuss the rules with children. Have them give you examples of why it is important to have these rules. The more they are involved, the more likely they are to follow the rules.

Hug Rug

Sometimes children simply need someone to show them they care. That can immediately calm them. Have a special hug rug. It can be a huge piece of laminated poster board with a big heart on it or a little mat. When children need a hug, they stand on the rug. That is a signal to other children that the child wants a hug. Some children do not like to be hugged or touched, and some states have licensing standards that preclude hugging. You can still use the hug rug. Depending on your state and its standards, here are three ways for children to get their hugs. The child and the hugger get to choose the way that feels best so long as it corresponds to state regulations.

1. Give a real hug.
2. Give a "pinky hug." Children hook their pinkies together.
3. Give a "talk hug." Children say, "I like you" to the child standing on the hug rug.

Figure 4.1 Hug Rug

Taking Pulse

When children start to get stressed, their pulse rates go up. Teach children to take their pulses. (Young children usually do not find it, but they have a good time trying.) When you see children are beginning to get upset, have them lower their pulses by five beats. Children sit quietly with their hands on their pulses and breathe deeply to calm themselves and lower their pulses. There may be times when you ask the entire class to calm down and lower their pulses by five beats.

Choosing Color

Another calming activity during the Trigger Stage is to have ten sheets of paper that are all different colors. When children feel angry, they browse through the colored sheets to find a calming color. When children find the most calming sheet of paper, they pull it out of the stack, sit down, and look at the paper while breathing deeply.

Talking About Feelings

One of my favorite strategies during this stage is to do what Mrs. Jenkins did with Tory. She had Tory talk about what was bothering him— his feelings about moving away. Talking provides an emotional release. Sometimes children need to talk right away. Set up a mini-conference area within your classroom. Two or three cozy chairs grouped around a table provide a safe area for children to go when they need to talk to you. If it is possible to listen to children at the time they are upset, do it. If it is not possible, have a special time each day for children to come and have a "mini-conference." They sign up in advance by putting their name cards (that have their individualized unique stickers) in the mini-conference box. Call their names to invite them to their mini-conference. Some children may choose not to come. They feel better because time has passed or because simply asking for the mini-conference was therapeutic. They no longer need to actually meet with you.

When having the mini-conference, use effective listening strategies. Be on the child's level. This helps the child feel safe. Sit comfortably facing the child. Make eye contact if you feel this is comfortable for the child. (There are some children who are uncomfortable with eye contact. It would defeat the purpose of the mini-conference.) Show that you are listening by nodding your head and focusing your attention on the child.

Your goal is to listen and learn and to allow children to come up with their own appropriate responses to situations that are upsetting. This empowers the children. Help children identify their choices and choose the most appropriate response.

Anger Options Chart

Have children create an anger options chart. This is a procedure that takes several days to fully implement. On the first day, gather the children around you and ask them all the things that make them angry. Record them all on a flip chart. When they are through, read them back to the children. Tell them the class will be working on this some more. The following day, ask the children all the ways they handle their anger. Write down all the ways they handle being mad. Afterward, read to them what you wrote. Tell them that they will be working on this some more. On the third day, start by reminding them about the anger rules: "It's OK to be angry, but it's not OK to hurt another child, property, yourself, or the teacher." Ask them which strategies they listed that comply with the anger rules. List these on a separate sheet called the anger options chart. Later, you can add some visuals so that they can "read" what was written. In the meantime, read them the anger options every day for several weeks as a reminder. When children are in Stage 1, the Trigger Stage, they can remember their options and know the most appropriate one for them.

Stage 2: The Turning Point Stage

I call this the Turning Point Stage because this is a turning point for angry children in determining how to express their anger. The primary emotion has been unresolved, and now they are almost ready to burst out in anger. This is a critical stage because it is your last chance to respond to the child's feelings in a way that facilitates communication and resolution. It is a stage in which it is still possible to reach children. There are strategies you can use to help children so that their anger does not escalate.

Push Pause Button

Children are very familiar with remote controls for their television sets. They know that each remote has a Play button and a Pause button. When they push thc Pause button on the remote, the program they are watching pauses. When they are ready to watch more, they push the Play button. Have a remote control in your classroom that is not connected to a television or other media. Remind children that it has a Pause button. Tell them that when they are feeling angry and want to explode, they can take the remote and push the Pause button. They continue to hold the Pause button while breathing deeply until they feel better. They then release the Pause button, push the Play button, and are ready to join the other children.

Mood Duster

Have a feather duster in your classroom. They are inexpensive and can often be purchased at dollar stores. Keep it in a special place. Explain that when a person becomes angry, the person often feels the anger everywhere. A way to calm down before saying or doing the wrong thing is to take the feather duster and "dust off" the anger. Demonstrate dusting yourself off gently with the feather duster. Children enjoy this simple yet effective strategy because it provides a visual for them to remove the anger from their minds and bodies. It's really cute to watch a child do it and then afterward say, "I feel all better now."

Relaxation Station

Have a cozy place in your classroom designated as the relaxation station. Add warm touches like a rocking chair, soft pillows, and relaxing pictures on the wall. Some teachers use landscapes or seascapes for the walls. Involve the children in choosing decorations for the relaxation station. Add some blank construction paper and crayons that children can use to draw their feelings. Add headphones with relaxing music for a nice finishing touch.

Limit the amount of time children spend in the relaxation station, or they will spend too much time there relaxing instead of becoming involved in classroom activities. Have a timer, and when the timer goes off, children return to their regular classroom routines. Some children will have to be redirected following the relaxation station to ensure that whatever they were doing was not the impetus that frustrated them in the first place.

Calming Bag

Create calming messages for children. Messages can say, "Push the Pause button" or "Go to the relaxation station." When children are upset, they reach into the calming bag and choose a folded message on how to cool down. They bring the message to you, you read it to them, and they follow the instructions. To make the calming bag even more special, have children tell you calming messages to place inside the bag. You can also take photos of the calming items and place them in the bag. Children reach in the bag and pull out a photo of one of the items like the mood duster, and then get the mood duster and calm themselves.

Turtle Time

Show the class a picture of a turtle. Discuss with the class what a turtle does when it is upset. Explain that when a turtle gets upset, it goes within its shell. Ask them to show you what that looks like with their body language. They generally tuck their head down on their desks, fold their arms, and tuck their feet under their chairs.

Talk about what happens when the turtle feels safe. Tell them that the turtle comes out of its shell. Have children demonstrate doing this too. Tell children that they can engage in this same strategy. When they feel angry and upset, they can say to themselves, "It is turtle time." They fold their arms, tuck their heads down, and take some deep breaths. When they are feeling calm again, they start moving around as they come out of their protective shells like a turtle. It is a very calming technique because it gives children permission to go within and calm down. This is a strategy that they will remember for their entire lives.

Stage 3: The Firing Stage

During this stage, children are so completely overwhelmed by anger and frustration that they lose the ability to think rationally. They have lost control. It's called the Firing Stage because they fire off, spouting off inappropriate words and behaviors. The target of this anger may be another child, school property, the teacher, or even themselves. They may lash out and hit someone or something. I have seen children bang their heads against a wall, try to pull their hair out, jump up on furniture, and try to hit teachers.

Caution Responding

This is not the time to try to reason with children. Don't touch them to calm them down because they may turn on you, and you may get hurt. Trying to approach children or talk to them during this phase only increases their frustration. They are in a critical phase and can't respond to what you are saying in a logical way. I have had older children who reported afterward that they didn't even remember what they said or did while they were in this stage.

Calming Mat

If you know that you have children who frequently have tantrums, have a special calming mat. When children become upset, they get the mat, lie down on it, and have their tantrum. When they are finished, they get back up and put away the mat.

Sammy had frequent tantrums. He used it as a vehicle to get what he wanted. It worked for him at home, so when he came into Ms. Gracie's class, he thought it would work there too. Ms. Gracie observed him and saw that this was his pattern. Even though she was careful to not give in when he had these tantrums, the tantrums continued because they were still working for him at home. One day, Ms. Gracie had a mini-conference with Sammy. She told him that it was fine with her if he had tantrums. He looked at her in surprise. She said she had a special mat for him that would help him become calmer and feel better. She went to a shelf and removed a small mat. She slowly and carefully unrolled it on the floor in an area where Sammy could not hurt himself if he had a tantrum. Up until that time, he had his tantrums anywhere by just dropping down on the hard floor and screaming and kicking.

She showed Sammy how he could get on the mat and have his tantrum. When he was through, he needed to get up and carefully roll up the calming mat and put it back on the shelf. She demonstrated how to do this. She had him practice taking the mat, putting it in its special place, and unrolling it. She then had him lie on it for a few seconds and then roll it back up and put it away. Later that same day, Sammy came to her and was very upset. He said, "Ms. Gracie, I'm getting the calming mat now." He went and got out the calming mat, unrolled it, had a tantrum, and then rolled it back up and put it away. He did this for several days that week and then eventually stopped having tantrums. They weren't working for him to get him what he wanted. Ms. Gracie shared the idea with Sammy's parents and they used it in their home too.

ABCD Technique

It's very important that you stay calm. The calmer you are, the calmer the children will be. Talk to the class calmly and reassure them. They will take their attitude from you.

The ABCD technique is an excellent way to become calm. The letters are used as a reminder for each of the four steps in the strategy.

A stands for "arrest yourself." Stop. If you say something in the heat of anger, you may regret it later.

B stands for "breathe." Take some deep breaths. When people become upset, they tend to breathe shallowly into their chests. This increases rather than decreases stress. Take a deep breath into your abdomen. Hold it for a few seconds and then slowly let it out. Do this several times.

C stands for "calming statements." Say calming statements to yourself. The words that you say to yourself about situations can profoundly change your attitude and then your actions. Say words like, "I am calm;" "I can handle this;" "I breathe deeply and become calmer and calmer."

D stands for "do it again." Do it over and over until you know that you are calm. Then, and only then, are you ready to act.

Stage 4: The Fall-Out Stage

After children have lost their tempers, they are typically exhausted from their own rage and anger. Some children do not even remember what they said or did in the heat of anger. Others may be embarrassed and experience remorse. Still others are glad that they expressed themselves and may even feel that others "had it coming." Now is the time to step in and ensure that this does not happen again.

Making Restitution

After the child calms down, it's time to do some damage control. If the child broke anything, it's important that the child finds a way to restore the property. This can take a long time. A good example of this is Adam, who was one of those adorable preschoolers with a great, mischievous smile, huge dark eyes, dark wavy hair, and an outgoing personality. He was frequently in trouble with his teacher. I was the director of the early childhood center at the time, and he was in and out of my office. One memorable morning, I walked into my office to find Adam. He stood there with a tiny bottle of white correction fluid in one hand and the brush from the bottle in the other hand. As I looked around my office, I quickly saw that my wooden desk was now decorated with white correction fluid. My black telephone had white dots. My computer had white streaks. My green Parsons table had white dots. I never knew there was so much correction fluid in such a tiny bottle!

Adam saw me and stood there, caught in the act. He started shaking and yelling, "I didn't do it! I didn't do it!" I was so upset that I could barely speak. I took some deep breaths and said in a low, deep voice, "You did do it, and now it needs to be fixed." He immediately threw himself on the floor and had one of the biggest tantrums I have seen in my years of teaching. He yelled, "I hate you! I hate this place!"

It took a while for Adam to become calm. When he was finally calm, we had a mini-conference. I said, "Do you want to tell me about it?" I did not ask, "Why did you do it?" I had learned over the years to never ask a child, "Why?" Children typically don't even realize why they do what they do. Sometimes they would rather make up a story than tell the truth. It's much better to ask, "Would you like to talk about it?" It's a good question that opens the door to more honest communication. Adam told me that he was mad at his mommy. He said she was mean because he wanted to stay in bed and she made him come to preschool. As we sat and talked, I was impressed by how articulate he was. When we both felt better, I told him that I still had a problem with all that white in my office. I asked him if he had any suggestions to make my office look good again. He told me he would clean it all up. Adam and I really bonded over the course of the next week as he cleaned off all the white correction fluid.

Making Amends

If the angry child hurts another child, it is important that the one who was angry make amends. This does not mean being forced to apologize. When children are forced to apologize and do not feel remorse, they are lying. They are learning to lie to get out of trouble. Amends is different. It is finding a way to make it up to the injured children. The children get together to discuss ways the angry child can make amends. It may be helping the injured child do a project. There have been children who have become good friends as a result of this intervention.

No Arguing

When children become calm, take charge and do not argue. Arguing turns into power struggles in which there are winners and losers. You are the teacher, and therefore you are in charge of the classroom. You have a choice—a choice whether or not you want to get into a struggle with a child.

When you get angry with children and allow them to push you over the edge, they learn that they can win. They can push your buttons. Once they learn they can push your buttons, they will continue to do so over and over again. It becomes a game for them called "get the teacher." The more frustrated you become, the more they enjoy the game.

Prearranged Signals

Have a mutually agreed-upon signal for children when they show signs of anger. The signal is a reminder to calm down. The signal can be something as simple as making the symbol of the peace sign by forming a V with the forefinger and middle finger. The signal can be given to only one child or to the entire class.

Calming Environment

Prevention of problems is a major goal. Look around at the classroom environment. Check out the colors in the room. Colors can carry a powerful message. There are some colors that are calming. Pink inhibits the release of hormones that contribute to aggressive behavior (Walker, 1991). It lowers blood pressure and rate of respiration. Have lots of pale pink in your room, especially in the relaxation station. Bring in a floor lamp from home or purchased at a garage sale. Add a pink bulb to the lamp to create a calming effect. You will find that it is especially effective in classes with children who are aggressive and unruly. Avoid having too much pink, as it is so calming that children will feel sleepy. At one seminar I gave in a hotel, my meeting room was changed to a restaurant. The restaurant was only open at night, and had pink lighting to create a better atmosphere. It was very difficult for me to keep my audience members awake because I, too, was so relaxed that I felt like taking a nap. A little pink lighting will go a long way.

Sky blue is another color that is calming for children. Blue fosters respect, responsibility, and knowledge (Wagner, 1985). Sky blue releases neurotransmitters that are calming to children.

One-on-One Solutions

Help children find ways to "not fire." They need to think about other strategies they can use in the future for becoming calm. What works once may not work the next time. Have them make their own individualized anger options charts. If they feel their anger escalating, they get out their charts and determine what will work best to regain self-control.

Self-Talk

Self-talk is what people say to themselves about any situation. People use it from the minute they get up in the morning until they go to bed at night. In the morning, self-talk might be something like, "It's raining outside. It's going to be a gloomy day." Self-talk occurs when you look in the mirror and say to yourself, "My hair looks great today. I really like the new gel I am using. I think I will buy more."

When angry, self-talk can be statements like, "I'm so mad. How could she do that to me? I feel like hitting something." Self-talk is effective for teaching children self-control (Kendall & Treadwell, 2007). Positive self-talk has words like, "I can handle this."

Teach children how to use self-talk. Start by demonstrating it. Talk about an upsetting situation and then make a self-talk statement appropriate to the age level: "I get out the mood duster and feel better." Do this about several different situations, changing the self-talk statement each time so that it is appropriate to the situation. They then role-play the situations, and instead of getting upset, they use self-talk.

OPPOSITIONAL DEFIANT DISORDER (ODD)

It is really important to be able to distinguish children who are angry from those who have oppositional defiant disorder (ODD). ODD is a chronic condition and creates major problems for those who have it and for the people in their lives. I am including it in this chapter even though it usually manifests in older children because I feel it is important for you to know and understand this disorder in case you ever encounter it.

One of my dearest friends married a man with ODD. He had told her that he had a Jekyll-and-Hyde personality, but hearing about it was not the same as living with it. When he was kind, he was very kind. When he raged, he really raged. She never knew when it was coming. She eventually divorced him. It took her months to recover from a marriage of walking on eggshells. She felt like she was on a roller coaster going up and down. His mother told her that he was like that from when he was a very little boy. That is what often happens in classrooms. Teachers have children with severe anger issues and do not realize that it is ODD. The teachers walk on eggshells, never knowing what to expect from these children.

ODD is a chronic, persistent, negative way of handling frustration, anxiety, and anger (American Psychiatric Association, 2000). It is persistent in that it has to last for at least six months before it can be called ODD. This is because people go through periods in their lives that can be difficult and they may react in strong ways that resemble ODD for short periods of time, but it eventually goes away. ODD does not go away.

Children with ODD handle their anger far differently from the way other children who are the same age and even from similar cultures handle anger. It is interesting that within classrooms, ODD does not immediately appear. Children with ODD may start out behaving appropriately, but once they get to know their teachers, they typically and frequently defy them and annoy both teachers and other children.

Children with ODD are quick to anger. Anything can set them off, so they go right to the "firing" stage. They are provocative and initiate confrontations with rudeness, lack of cooperation, and general resistance to those in authority (see more symptoms of ODD in Figure 4.2). There are specific medications that can be used for ODD, as well as classroom strategies. Some of the strategies you have learned in this chapter will also help you with children with ODD.

Medical Management

This is a very real disorder, and there are medications that are beneficial. I have personally seen the difference they can make in children with ODD.

Moods Are Contagious

It's important that you remain calm even when children are provocative. They know exactly how to push your buttons. Even if they succeed in provoking you inside, do not let them see it on the outside. I often say at seminars, "Fake it until you make it." Your mood is contagious, more contagious than a cold, so stay calm. Your mood will set the tone for the entire class.

Figure 4.2 Symptoms of Oppositional Defiant Disorder

Symptoms of Oppositional Defiant Disorder

- Easily annoyed and irritated
- Easily frustrated
- Ignores directions
- Dislikes rules
- Refuses to comply with requests
- Disobeys authority
- Argumentative
- Persistently insists on having own way
- Defiant
- Deliberately annoys others
- Blames others for mistakes
- Sensitive
- Lack of ability to be flexible
- High maintenance
- Sees things in terms of black and white
- Outbursts
- Difficulty controlling temper
- May break or destroy things when angry
- May harm self when angry
- May use obscene language
- Moody
- Extremely compliant about some issues
- Has Jekyll-and-Hyde personality
- Negative

Signals

Develop signals ahead of time. Children with ODD are generally very strong willed, so for the signals to be most effective, they need to choose them. The more involved they are, the more invested they will be in having the signals work.

Anger Options Chart

Ask them for ways they can remain calm even when they feel provoked. The anger options chart is effective. When they make their own individual options charts, they are once again most invested in having it work.

Appropriate Expressions

Children do not know it, but they are often starved for ways to express themselves. When they don't know appropriate ways, they engage in inappropriate ways. I was once called in on a consultation, but instead of just observing to help the teacher, I met with the children. They were great! They told me their behavior issues. They were each aware of them. I then offered suggestions. It was a wonderful experience because the entire class chipped in to help each other and these young children knew what would work for them and what would not work. Several of the children had problems with aggressive behavior. They did not know how to deal with situations that aroused feelings of frustration, hurt, and disappointment. I gave them as a class lessons in social skills. You can do this too.

Asking for Wants and Needs

When children do not know how to ask for what they want, they may act out. They need appropriate wording. Teach them to say, "I would appreciate . . . " when asking for something. Have them role-play asking for what they want, "I would appreciate you sharing the puzzles with me." This gives them a way of asking respectfully, rather than getting argumentative or combative.

Positive Expectations

The more you believe in children, the more they will believe in themselves. Teach them to think positively about what they can do. Some children feel like failures. They have been told over and over again that they are "bad" and out of control. Talk about the fact that what occurred in the past can stay in the past. They can start over again. Give them hope that they can succeed. Most of all, remember this is a real psychological disorder. If you see signs, it is important to seek help for this child.

How to Handle Bullying

5

Sticks and stones and words can break bones of the body and the spirit.
                                                              —Maryln Appelbaum

---

Bullying has become more and more of a problem in recent years. Fifteen percent of children are either bullies or victims of bullies. It doesn't matter if preschools are large or small, the ethnic composition of the school, or the school setting. Bullying can and does occur in all settings (Banks, 1997).

RECOGNIZING BULLYING

A bully is defined as someone who repeatedly harms others over time through direct attacks like teasing, taunting, threatening, and hitting or through indirect attacks like spreading rumors, intentional exclusion, and social isolation. Boys generally use more direct attacks, while girls use more indirect bullying methods. At seminars I hear increasingly that girls are now engaging in more direct physical attacks, too.

Bullying can occur by one person, or there may be a team of people all involved in bullying one or more victims. Children who are targeted all have in common that they are physically, verbally, or socially weaker than the bully (Hazler, as cited by Carney & Merrell, 2001).

Children who are bullies generally need to feel powerful and in control. They seem to obtain satisfaction from inflicting suffering on others and have very little empathy. When questioned about bullying, they think their behavior was reasonable and defend their actions, saying that their victims provoked them. Bullies typically display no anxiety about what they are doing. They may lie to defend themselves, steal, taunt, and show cruelty to animals ("Bullies and Their Victims," 2001).

Bullying can be difficult to detect. Children who are victims are often frightened to "tell" on the bully. I have noticed some recurrent themes in children who bully. They often engage in play that has violent themes. They are often the children who try to take over the classroom. For example, Camden was in Ms. Jessie's class. She said that he sat directly opposite her at circle time and tried to turn the attention of the children on himself. He consistently wanted things his way and refused to follow directions. When he was disappointed or felt criticized in any way, he reacted by becoming extremely angry and blaming others.

Those are traits that I too have seen in children who bully others. I have also observed that they draw other children around them who are aggressive too. The characteristic I have observed that I find the most disturbing is a lack of empathy for others. I have heard stories of preschoolers who not only lack empathy for other children, but also for animals. One little boy took took several goldfish out of the fishbowl and squeezed them to hurt them. Another child bragged that he tried to put his cat in the microwave to cook him. At one center, I was told of a 5-year-old boy who constantly bullied others. One day, he snuck into the younger children's playground and tried to strangle a 3-year-old girl.

Victims of Bullying

Victims of bullying are not the popular social butterflies of the school; rather, they are the opposite. They are typically anxious and insecure, lack social skills, have few friends, and feel socially isolated. They rarely defend themselves, and they rarely retaliate. Bullying can lead victims to feel depressed, lower their self-esteem, and carry over into adulthood. There are some children who are so victimized that they plan and carry out acts of retribution against not only bullies, but also others. An example of this with older children is the shootings at Columbine High School, where the shooters had been victimized for years and had reached the point where they wanted to strike back. Columbine and other school shootings involving victims of bullying clearly demonstrate the immensity of the problem.

Bullying impacts the bully, the victim, and everyone else who is involved. There is a strong correlation that exists between being a bully during school years and experiencing legal or criminal trouble as an adult. Sixty percent of children who bully in middle school have at least one criminal conviction by the time they are 24 years old (Olweus, as cited by Banks, 1997). Children who chronically bully others usually also bully when they are adults, having a negative impact on their lives. Developing warm and caring positive relationships is difficult because others withdraw from chronic bullies. And this all may have started in early childhood.

STRATEGIES FOR UNDERSTANDING AND HANDLING BULLYING

Bullying has to be nipped in the bud. The way to do this is to ensure that bullying interventions involve the entire preschool, not just the perpetrator and victim. Programs for both bullies and their victims must be in place, and those who are victims need to learn that they do not have to remain victims (Dess, 2001).

Start your anti-bullying program by having a bully-free classroom. Have class discussions about bullying. Ask children, "Do you know what bullying means? Has anyone ever felt like someone was being mean to them? How did that feel? How do you think bullies feel? What's it like to watch someone get bullied? Who would like to have a bully-free classroom?" Then discuss having a bully-free classroom. Establish some rules to set the tone for a classroom that is bully-free. Children all offer suggestions for those rules (Beane, 1999). Examples of those rules can include

- We treat each other with respect.
- We speak up if we see others being treated unfairly.
- We like it that people are all different.
- We treat each other the way we want to be treated.
- We like to feel safe.

The best way to have a bully-free classroom is to have a total prevention program. Have a "starlights classroom" to teach children to act kindly toward others. Call the children "starlights." Have each child's picture in the center of a big star on a poster. Talk about how stars shining down make you feel good when you see them. Tell them, "In our classroom, we want everyone to feel good. Everyone shines like starlight."

Starlight Acts

Talk about doing acts of kindness—"starlight acts." Explain that an act of kindness is something that makes others feel good. Give them a few examples of acts of kindness. "Megan helped me clean up the classroom." "Jory gave me a huge smile." "Grayson helped Todd put away all of the blocks." Then ask the children to tell you other acts of kindness that others in their classroom have done.

Starlight Acts

Get out a box filled with tiny sticky stars. Tell the children that every time they do something nice for someone else—a "starlights act"—you will put a star up on the starlight poster that has all their pictures. A starlight act is an act of kindness that helps other children shine and feel better. The object is to fill up the whole poster board with little stars surrounding the big stars—the starlight children. Involve the parents. Children bring notes from home about starlight acts that they did. The parents can have their own "starlights charts."

Starlights Hug Time

At a seminar I showed a video clip of a man who wore a sign saying, "Free hugs." At first everyone around the man looked at him like he was crazy, but then one woman went up to him and let him hug her, and soon everyone wanted hugs. The movement grew and others started wearing signs saying, "Free hugs." I do not know whether this whole thing was staged, but I do know that the people sure looked happy. My audience was a group of early childhood educators. I told them that they could walk around the room and give each other hugs—either regular hugs or thumb hugs or just big smiles. Everyone did this, and they were so happy. This was early in the morning, and it created a very warm atmosphere for the entire day. I don't think I have ever had so many audience members come up to me all day and give me so many hugs. The point is that children enjoy having a special time each day in which they can hug each other. The hugs can be regular hugs or thumb or even pinky hugs, or just wonderful warm smiles. As they do it, tell them to pretend they are like real stars in the sky, shining their light on their friends as they hug them.

Starlights "New Friend" Day

A good way to ensure that children get to know each other in positive ways is to help children meet and get to know each other. Otherwise, they often just play with the same children over and over, and it is easy for a child to feel excluded. That is the child that can become the victim of teasing. To prevent this from happening, once a week pair children with a new starlight friend. Have them start the day by holding hands and saying, "Hi, Starlight Friend," and then give each other one of the forms of hugs (Sprung, Froschi, & Hinitz, 2005). They play together, and at the end of day, they draw a picture as a gift for their new friend.

Starlight Friends Treats

Have the children each bring in a small baggie of their favorite snacks. Send home a list of acceptable foods for the snacks. This will ensure that children who have any type of allergies do not get something they cannot eat. Mix all of the "starlight treats" together in a bowl and serve them for snack. Teach the children how different things go together to make something good. Some of the treats are big, and some are small. They are all different but when they are put together, they make something wonderful. Explain to the children that they each look and act differently too. Some children are small, others are tall; some are thin, others are bigger; some have light skin, others have darker skin; some learn things quickly, some take a little longer; some have great memories, some are better at doing things with their hands. Everyone is different, just like in the "starlight treats." They each are special in their own way and together, they are a wonderful class, just like together, the starlight treats are great.

Starlight Songs

Every day sing fun songs and call them "starlight songs." Sing songs about friendship, kindness, and caring.

Be a Role Model

It's important for all children that you are a role model demonstrating positive behaviors. It is even more important for children who bully. When children see you as a calm, positive, and patient, yet firm and strong, role model, they will emulate that behavior.

Control Media Input

Children's brains are like recorders taking in all that they see around them. Encourage families to limit the amount of television their children watch. When their children do watch television, have families monitor the programs to ensure they are not watching violent programming. Children often copy some of their television heroes. Nicky loved to watch television at home. Ms. Ashley, his teacher, noticed that whenever he wore a T-shirt with a picture of a television character that was always fighting, Nicky fought. Those were the days he bullied and hit others the most. She tried an experiment one day. He had a change of clothes at the preschool, and she asked him to change into a different T-shirt. It was a plain one. Within a few minutes, he grew calmer. She talked to his parents and asked them to make sure he didn't wear that T-shirt anymore. It seems that he had more than one! She also asked them to work with her to control the programs he watched on television. They did, and slowly but gradually his behavior changed. Media makes a big difference. At times, it seems to me that media has taken over for parents as role models for children because so many children seem to spend more time in front of a television than they do with their busy parents.

Teach Assertive Skills

When a child does something that seems mean, often the victim does not stand up and say anything. Instead, the victim tries to hide and hopes it will stop. Teach children to stand up for themselves in positive ways. If children feel hurt, teach them to say, "I don't like it when you do that. Stop."

Have them practice this over and over again. Some children, especially shy and quiet children, have to practice this many times. I have used role-plays and we take turns being the one to say, "I don't like it when you do that. Stop." They sometimes change the words to fit their own unique personalities, and that is fine. The important thing is that it is said calmly and assertively.

Teach children to ask for help from you when they need it. That is part of being assertive too, to say, "Can you help me?" They need to feel safe to come to you to ask you to intervene.

Role-Plays

I mentioned role-plays in being assertive. Do them with the entire class. Role-plays are a powerful method for teaching new behaviors. Victims and those who watch bullying without doing anything about it (bystanders) all learn new skills for handling bullying. Make up stories for the role-plays. Include bullies engaged in bullying, a victim, and bystanders watching the bullying. Figure 5.1 show a sample role-play that you can use with your class.

Posture

Children who are victims are generally not the type of children who stand up for themselves with their words or in their stature. Teach them how to walk tall. Have them practice standing straight and walking. Provide activities that hook their interest to help them feel better about themselves. Assign them peer buddies so they don't feel lonely. The goal is to help them feel better about themselves and to have them walk tall.

Developing Leaders

Children who bully others are often natural leaders. One of the ways that you can help them stop bullying is to rechannel their leadership ability so that they engage in positive acts rather than negative ones. Here is a story to illustrate this point. I will never forget Vinny. I was the director of a preschool, and he was one of the children enrolled. Vinny was very tall for his age, muscular, and had long, dark, slicked-back hair and dark

Figure 5.1 Sample Role-Play

Sample Role-Play

Four-year-old Alex was very short for his age and wore big glasses. One day he was on the playground watching the other children. They were playing around him. Two taller boys came up to him and started barking like mean dogs. Alex did not know what to do. He nervously giggled. One of the children said, "Hey, stupid, that is what you are. You are a dog." Alex could barely breathe. He felt like he could hear the pounding of his heart. The two children kept on barking, and then they started making comments about how short Alex was, calling him a "little squirt." They made fun of his height, short legs, and thick glasses. Alex was too scared to tell them to stop. He wished he was safe at home. Other kids were watching. Some came over and watched and one child even joined in the bullying. Finally, it was time to go inside. Alex was scared the rest of the day. He was too scared to go to the restroom for fear one of those kids would come in. He could hardly wait to go home. He felt like crying, but was embarrassed and held it in.

Questions for Children

If you were on the playground and overheard this, what could you do to help Alex?

Does Alex have to go through this bullying because he is shorter?

How do you think Alex feels?

Has this ever happened to you?

What are some things that Alex could have done?

What do you think of the children who bullied Alex?

How could you help the children who were bullies to never bully again?

What can you say to someone who bullies you?

eyes. He was a natural leader. He had other children gathered around him wherever he went. They sat near him in learning centers and wanted to be with him during outside playtime. I noticed that children were around him but some seemed scared of him. I also started noticing that there were some children who avoided him altogether on the playground. One day I discovered why. I found Vinny bullying Howie, a child who was very tiny for his age, was shy, and stuttered when he spoke. I broke up the bullying and when I investigated, I discovered that this was not the first time. I also discovered that Vinny had bullied a few other children.

I knew I had to do something. After thinking about it for a few days, I had a private mini-conference with Vinny. I said, "You know, Vinny, I have been watching you. I see that other children listen to you." He nodded his head in agreement. I continued, "I think you have natural leadership ability. The kids all listen to you when you speak in and outside the classroom." Vinny again nodded his head in agreement. He was more and more interested in what I had to say. I said, "I would like to work with you and develop your leadership ability. I think you can go on to become a real leader. Who knows, you might become mayor, senator, or even president some day." Vinny listened even more attentively. I told him, "I would like to give you a role in the classroom, a time each day during circle time when you get to start practicing your leadership. How does that sound to you?" Vinny nodded his head. He was totally absorbed in this conversation. I continued, "Great. That is what we will do. Of course, as a leader, you will have to be a role model of correct behavior so that others learn to copy that behavior. That's what leaders do—inspire others to do the right thing. That's the kind of leader I want to help you be. Is that OK with you?" Vinny nodded his head and agreed. And that was the start of a whole new way of behaving for Vinny. We involved the class, telling them that he was a leader-in-training. At first, some children may have been frightened, but soon they really enjoyed this new side of Vinny. He had channeled his leadership abilities into something positive.

There's an even greater ending to this story. Vinny and I stayed in touch not only through preschool, but also all through elementary school and then secondary school. He invited me to his high school graduation and, later on, his college graduation. I was invited to his home following the graduation ceremony. He showed me his scrapbooks and how he had been named most likely to succeed. He was president of his senior class. He proudly talked about his accomplishments to me, and then he said, "But you know, I will never be elected president of the United States." I said, "Why not, Vinny?" He said, "Because I am foreign-born." I told him, "Vinny, for you, they will change the laws." You just never know how the words you say can make a difference in the lives of children. He had remembered my words to him from so long ago. That is what you can do, too. You, too, can inspire children to be better, to channel the leadership abilities that they are using to bully, to instead be positive leaders. Every day you get to make a difference in the lives of children. You are a difference maker.

How to Handle Children With Bipolar Disorder

6

Teachers are the anchors for students on the ship called Hope.
—Maryln Appelbaum

A t a meeting of one of the local psychological associations, the speaker was a top-notch psychiatrist who has been conducting research on bipolar disorder and depression. I had already learned much about bipolar disorder, and I was interested in what he had to say. When I first started learning about bipolar disorder many years ago, it was said that people do not show any symptoms until the age of 18. (In those days, it was called manic depressive disorder.) In recent years, however, bipolar disorder has inched its way up to being a frequently diagnosed disorder in young children. I was very interested in what the psychiatrist thought about this. He spoke about symptoms and about the newest medications. He answered a few questions. He did not address bipolar disorder in young children. I approached him afterward and asked him what he thought about children being diagnosed with this disorder. He told me that just as with ADHD, he believed that while many diagnoses were valid, many were invalid.

WHAT IS BIPOLAR DISORDER?

It is true that there are some children with bipolar disorder, but as I describe to you the symptoms, I want you to know that it takes a professional to make the diagnosis, and even then, they can make an error. There is a lot of discussion in the world about racial profiling, an assumption that all people who share a similar race are the same. There is no talk in the world about psychological profiling, assuming that every child or adult that shares similar characteristics actually has a disorder. Be cautious in how you approach children who you suspect have this or any other disorder. There are some psychologists and psychiatrists who believe that it does not truly exist in children (Smith, 2001). There may be a variety of reasons why children act as they do. I know that I am not at my very best when I don't take care of myself, sleep enough, eat well, or when I am under stress. For some children, it could be as simple as that. For other children, it could be a real disorder. Twenty to sixty percent of adults with bipolar disorder report having had some symptoms as children (Smith, 2001).

The diagnosis is often complicated by the fact that many children with bipolar disorder have ADHD. Some symptoms of the two disorders overlap, including motor restlessness, distractibility, difficulty following through on tasks or directions, interrupting, and lack of attention to details (Jimenez, 2000). Some children with bipolar disorder are diagnosed as having ADHD and are treated with stimulant medication. If these children have bipolar disorder, the stimulant medication may make them more manic.

It is very important to have an accurate diagnosis (Duffy, 2007) because children with bipolar disorder can suffer serious consequences if they do not receive appropriate medical treatment. Children may engage in reckless behavior, which may lead to self-injury, hospitalization, and even attempted suicide. Moreover, without treatment, children will have difficulties in both their home and school relationships because of their reckless behaviors and mood swings.

Signs of bipolar disorder can begin as early as infancy. Babies may be more difficult to care for and less predictable. As these children grow older, they may have severe separation anxiety and extreme moodiness and irritability. They engage in disruptive behavior that gets worse and worse along with temper tantrums and an inability to handle frustration. Outsiders look at their behaviors and find them strange and extremely emotional and cannot figure out why their moods change for no discernable reason. As children swing between high-energy mania and depression, you may notice extreme moodiness and irritability that is very visible and disruptive for the classroom.

While many children are talkative, children with bipolar disorder in the manic phase talk a lot and talk differently (Biederman et al., 2000). They use pressured speech, speaking extremely rapidly, firing off one thought after another, and it's difficult to keep up with what they are saying. The speech may or may not make sense, as they often illogically jump from one idea to another as their thoughts race together.

I was recently asked to consult with David. He was a really nice looking child with a great smile, a happy attitude, and lots of enthusiasm. I asked him what he was interested in, and that was all it took for him to launch into a long talk. He started telling me about building something in his room, then jumped to getting his parents to buy the wood and how expensive it was, how he loves to eat steak, how cows are sometimes too skinny, and that he has been sick lately and his doctor said he has something called bipolar disorder, but he doesn't want to take the pills, and he hopes his family doesn't catch his house on fire because once he set the house on fire. He said all of this within minutes. As I sat there listening to his pressured speech, I felt my heart go out to this bright child. I asked him why he wouldn't take his medicine, and he cited what I have heard so often. He didn't like how he felt when he took it. He said, "It doesn't feel like me. I hate it."

During periods of mania, children generally behave as David did. They are in constant motion and frequently restless. He could not sit still. His foot was constantly moving. When he talked about setting his house on fire, he was demonstrating yet another characteristic of bipolar disorder; children with this disorder may engage in daring feats of behavior that can cause harm to themselves and to others. They may believe they are unstoppable, like they can do anything. I had an acquaintance whose husband was diagnosed with bipolar disorder. He thought he could fly and jumped off the top level of an atrium hotel to his death. This is a serious disorder and must be treated so that lives can be saved.

Children with bipolar disorder have drastic mood changes, sometimes rapidly, between being manic and then sinking into deep depression. The depressive states are totally the opposite of feeling manic. They are debilitating. They are characterized by persistent sadness, worrying, anxiety, and lack of energy for normal activities. Children can barely get up in the morning and may have a "Who cares?" attitude. They can't concentrate or make decisions because everything seems so overwhelming. They withdraw from friendships and other relationships. The depression may be expressed as anger, irritability, and agitation. Children may have recurring thoughts of death and suicide. In fact, suicide is a real threat in individuals with bipolar disorder. See Figure 6.1 for a checklist of early signs of bipolar disorder.

When adults have bipolar disorder, they may stay in a manic state or a depressive state for days or weeks before cycling. Children, on the other hand, can cycle rapidly between manic and depressive states, often in minutes or hours. This makes it hard not only on the teacher and other children who never know what to expect, but also on the children who feel they have no control over their emotions. They are correct. They do not have control over their emotions. This makes living with bipolar disorder a very painful and lonely experience.

Figure 6.1 Checklist of Early Signs of Bipolar Disorder

Checklist of Early Signs of Bipolar Disorder

- ☐ Unpredictable
- ☐ Severe separation anxiety
- ☐ Violently dislikes transitions and new situations
- ☐ Temper tantrums
- ☐ Increasing behavior problems
- ☐ Extreme moodiness
- ☐ Extreme irritability
- ☐ Sleep problems
- ☐ Aggression followed by remorse
- ☐ Impulsive
- ☐ Lack of concentration
- ☐ Inability to handle frustration
- ☐ Hyperactivity
- ☐ Extremely emotional
- ☐ Mood swings
- ☐ Delusional thinking

STRATEGIES FOR SUCCEEDING WITH CHILDREN WITH BIPOLAR DISORDER

Medical Management

The first step in managing this disorder is to get an accurate diagnosis and start the child on medication that can help the child have control over mood swings. The medication used for bipolar disorder is typically a mood stabilizer and sometimes an anti-depressant. This medication needs to be taken on a regular, consistent basis. Frequently children with bipolar disorder do not like taking their medication. Like what happened with David, children start taking the medicine and do not like its calming effects. They are used to the "highs" of mania and don't like the new way they feel. Additionally, families may see that their children are behaving better, so they think their children are cured and stop giving them the medication. Children feel so good that they too think they are cured. The symptoms then reoccur. Medical care needs to be consistent, and medication needs to be monitored. Because children are so young, it's always important that families do research on the effects of all medication on the developing brain.

Structure

Children with bipolar disorder need structure. They need consistency and routine to reduce the opportunity for mood swings. Watch out for unplanned changes in routine, as this can trigger a mood change.

Mood Diary

Because mood swings are a constant problem, it is useful for you to track children's moods. Keep a mood diary so you can predict their moods. A pattern may emerge that will help prevent mood swings. Record each day's major events and their moods afterward. It is sometimes possible to predict the mood swings. Kim felt tired, and she said her thoughts felt like they were in slow motion right before she became depressed. Caleb became talkative, speaking rapidly, and that was a cue that he was about to go into a manic state. Some children cannot see their own cues, but you will begin to see a pattern emerge when you have a mood diary.

Cozy Retreat

When children are particularly irritable and emotional, a cozy retreat can help calm them. One of my favorite ways to create a really quiet, cozy retreat was to take a table, put it in a quiet area of the room, pop a few cozy pillows under it, and partially cover it with a nice frilly tablecloth. Children liked it so much that I had to set up some rules about it. I placed a liquid timer next to the pillows and told children that they could flip the three-minute timer two times before they had to come back into the classroom. (If children were having a really bad day, they could come to me to negotiate a longer stay.) I also had the "one child, one bracelet" rule. I attached a little hook to the table and hung a woven bracelet on it. When children wanted to go into the retreat, they put on the bracelet. This was a signal to other children that someone was already on retreat. When a child finished being in the retreat, the bracelet had to go back on the hook so other children could take a turn.

Goal Setting

Goals help children stay focused. Have children set goals. Write them down. The goals have to be something they really want. Just having that goal in sight can help them through the ups and downs of this disorder. It helps them feel they can succeed. It gives them a purpose.

Sleep

Getting proper sleep is important for everyone, but it is especially important in maintaining mood stability. Even individuals without bipolar disorder have a hard time functioning without sleep. Children with bipolar disorder may have extreme mood fluctuations if they go two or more nights without sleep.

Offering Hope

Have you ever gone through a tough time when you felt like you could not control your mood? I have. In one year, my mom, my best friend, and my little dog all passed away. I thought I handled it pretty well, but sometimes, I just would see something or hear something that reminded me of a loved one, and I would get really sad and sometimes start to cry. I did not plan to get sad. It just happened. What got me through this period was the caring of the other people in my life. Imagine being a child with bipolar disorder and not being in control of your moods. They, too, need lots of support and encouragement.

All children are sensitive to the words you use. Positive words are much more effective than negative. Use positive wording with children and avoid anything that can make them feel bad for their moodiness. Bipolar disorder is a real illness. It cannot be seen like a broken limb or glasses or a hearing aid. It can only be seen in the moods of the children. It's important to stay positive so that they, too, can stay positive.

Pet Care

If it's at all possible, have pets in the classroom. When children take care of pets and hold and hug them, it is soothing. If your preschool does not allow live pets, substitute a class stuffed animal. Give the stuffed animal a name and make it come to life for the children. They can have special clothes for it for different seasons. They can take turns taking it home on weekends and journal their activities with their new friend. Even older children enjoy having that stuffed animal. They may laugh and be silly when introduced to their new friend, but it is amazing how much of a difference it can make.

Stop Sign

Make stop signs out of construction paper. Children can help color the octagon. Write the word "stop" in the center. Place the stop signs near children who need to calm down. Make sure they are in a place where the children can easily see them. They serves as a visual cue to take some deep breaths and calm down.

Movement

Children need to move when they are feeling restless. Send them on errands, even within the classroom. "Jemitha, I need you to carry this book over to that shelf. Thank you so much."

Stressbusters

Involve the class in some stretches to get exercise and provide movement. Do some deep breathing together as a class. Play calming music or fun music—music that is mood changing. The less stress children experience, the better they can feel.

Outside Help

Finally, if all of these strategies on any given day are not enough and you see that children are getting either very manic or appear really depressed, they may need extra help. A change may need to be made in medication or the dosage. Severe depression is very serious. In younger children, it can manifest as anger as well as turning inward. In older children and adults, it can lead to suicide.

Suicide is a real threat for those with bipolar disorder. I have not heard of many cases in preschoolers; however, it does happen with older children. If a child talks or hints about suicide, take it seriously. I vividly remember the first time I heard a child talk about suicide. I was working as a therapist at the time in a clinic. I immediately reported it to the head psychologist, and it turned out that this child had already plotted out the details of how he was going to take his life. That one action saved his life. Be vigilant. You can help save a life. Look for other symptoms, including withdrawing from friends, an inability to concentrate, dramatic changes in personal appearance, and loss of interest in favorite activities. Watch also for expressions of hopelessness and guilt, preoccupation with death, and giving away favorite possessions. If you see any of these symptoms, get immediate help for these children. You may be helping to save lives.

How to Handle Children With Autism Spectrum Disorder

7

I can remember rarely hearing about children with autism spectrum disorder (ASD). That has dramatically changed in recent years. In 2000, when the American Psychiatric Association wrote about autism, they cited the incidence as five cases in ten thousand. Now it is estimated to affect one child in every one hundred fifty (Jepson, 2007). That is a dramatic increase, which is why it is important for everyone who works with children with ASD to be armed with both an understanding of this disorder as well as classroom strategies to help children.

WHAT IS AUTISM SPECTRUM DISORDER?

ASD falls under the umbrella of a disorder known as pervasive developmental disorder (PDD). There are distinct characteristics of all individuals with PDD. They all have severe problems with social interactions and communication skills and typically also have maladaptive atypical behaviors not commonly seen in others (American Psychiatric Association, 2000).

Children with ASD have a triad of deficits in social reciprocity, communication, and repetitive behaviors or interests. All of these can range from mild to severe. They affect the ability of children to communicate, have social interactions, and perform in an educational setting (Stuart, Flis, & Rinaldi, 2006). You can usually see this in the classroom in delays or abnormal functioning in language and in social interactions.

One of the most amazing facts about ASD is that in 20 percent of families, children started out with language skills and seemingly normal social interactions (Jepson, 2007). Then, sometime in the first or second year, children either stop talking or start engaging in unusual behaviors. I have spoken to many stunned parents. They tell me that they had no idea there was any problem, that their children were fine, and then, *wham*, their children seemed to totally change. It is heartbreaking to hear the stories from these families. Still, other families saw problems right from the start and say that there was never a normal period of development.

The symptoms of this disorder are different in all children, who fall on a spectrum of mild to severe. The spectrum may include mental retardation that also ranges from mild to severe. Children with ASD are almost always more interested in objects than in people. This is characterized by a persistent preoccupation with objects that can include buttons, paper clips, rubber bands, and pencils. If the object moves, they may be even more fascinated by it. They may become preoccupied with fans or spinning wheels on toy cars. Kyle was one of those children. He was totally absorbed by the wheels on toy cars. He sat for hours, spinning them back and forth. He also liked boxes and jars. He would open them and then close them, open them and close them, over and over again. Some children's fascination with objects extends to their own bodies. They become preoccupied with their belly buttons, arms, or legs. They may swing their arms back and forth or in a circle repeatedly.

Another typical behavior is an insistence on sameness. Even the smallest change in the environment can provoke a tantrum. It can be as small as changing the time by five minutes for lunch, lining up at a different place to go outside, or changing the silverware used at lunchtime.

Children with ASD also have a need for repetition. Just like a spinning object, that same need for repetition is shown in other behaviors. They may again and again line up a group of objects for no apparent reason. They may repeatedly imitate the actions of someone in their lives or even of an actor they saw on television. Their hands may flap repeatedly, their fingers may flick, or they may clap their hands repeatedly. They rock back and forth or sway. This can look even more unusual because of odd body postures like walking on tiptoe or stooping while walking.

All of these behaviors can profoundly impact their relationships with peers. They generally lack eye contact, are not spontaneous, and have an inability to share in fun and even the achievements of others. They often need help in developing peer relationships.

Their speech may be delayed or nonexistent. Even if they do speak, the rate, tone, and pitch of their speech may not sound normal. Their grammar may be immature, and their speech may be filled with repetitive words, words that do not fit the conversation. Moreover, their words generally do not match their gestures and body movement. They may not understand directions you give or questions you ask. This deficit in language and communication skills can be a huge hindrance to their development.

This is a devastating disorder for so many families. I recently spoke to one mother of a boy with autism. She told me how her son had started developing normally. He made eye contact, was affectionate, and was starting to speak. When he was nearly 1 year old, he started to be more fascinated with objects and stopped making eye contact. He did not want to be held or touched anymore. His language not only stopped progressing, but it went backwards. This mom found herself in the autism loop, trying to get help for her son and desperate for some answers. This desperation occurs in many families. The children need your support and so, too, do the families. The children leave you at the end of the day and at the end of the school year, but the families have them forever and need all the help they can get for these very special children. The good news is that effective strategies do exist. You can also teach those strategies to families so that they can use them at home. The more you are a team, the better for your classroom and the better for parents and their children.

Before proceeding to strategies for ASD, there is something very important you need to know. There are children who are diagnosed with ASD who do not have it. Instead, they have Reactive Attachment Disorder (RAD; Mukaddes, Bilge, Alyanak, & Kora, 2000). The symptoms of RAD can be very similar to those I have described for ASD. The onset is prior to five years of age, just as in children with ASD. Some of these symptoms include language impairment, cognitive delays, motor delays, lack of eye contact, little interest in people, lack of social appropriateness, and stereotypical behaviors like head banging, rocking, and flapping arms—all similar to ASD. However, while we currently are unsure about the cause of ASD, there is certainty about the cause of RAD.

Bowlby was the first to recognize attachment disorders more than 50 years ago in children who had been hospitalized (Bowlby, 1980, as cited in Allan, Hauser, Borman-Spurrell, 1996). In those days parents were not allowed to stay with their children. In fact, they could only visit them infrequently. At first the children cried because they missed their mothers. After a while, they did not seem to care if their mothers came or did not visit them. These same children went on to have symptoms. These studies of attachment disorders were carried further, and it was found that children who were at home with their mothers could still develop RAD. (In those days it was more common for the mother to be the stay-at-home parent.) They found this in cases in which mothers were withdrawn from their children. Some of the mothers suffered from depression and were unavailable for the bonding their children needed. RAD is generally tied to maltreatment and/or neglect (Schwartz, 2006).

Mukaddes et al. (2000) did a study of children who had been diagnosed with ASD, but who really had RAD. They found that when they interviewed the parents, 80 percent of these children were exposed to intensive television viewing for approximately seven hours every day. When interviewing parents, they also found that many of these children were left alone for as much as five hours a day. Just as children with ASD may have started out with apparently normal development, so too did these children. Their development also changed and became arrested or regressed. Interestingly, the treatment for these children was teaching their parents new behaviors to use with their children over a three-month period. As they bonded with their children, the children markedly improved. This is very different from children with ASD. Children with RAD have the capacity for normal social and cognitive development. Because they have this capacity, when they are given early appropriate care, they respond.

Children with ASD also need love and bonding. However, that is not enough to help them recover. They need the strategies you will now be learning.

STRATEGIES FOR SUCCEEDING WITH CHILDREN WITH ASD

Structure

Once again, it is vital to have structure. Children with ASD thrive on sameness, routine, and consistency. Any change in the schedule or routine can result in maladaptive behavior, ranging from a mild tantrum to head banging.

Consistent Routines

Use systematic and consistent ways of carrying out tasks. It helps to have a routine of "first work, then play." The children get used to having the fun activities after the work activities. Routines help to minimize memory and attention problems. Children always know what to expect and when to expect it. Routines also have the bonus of helping children compensate for their language delays. They do not have to ask or be told what to do. They know. They have learned the routine, and they know what to do and when to do it.

Left to Right, Top to Bottom

This drive for sameness extends to everything, including the layout of shelves in the classroom. Have items in learning centers in sequential order of use from left to right and from top to bottom. This prepares them for reading because books are written in this format, top to bottom and left to right.

Clear Visual Areas

Children with ASD are easily distracted, and it's important if you want children to concentrate on a task to have an area free of all distractions. Choose an area of the classroom for seating that is simplified to minimize distractions. Have individualized study carrels, but ensure that the children do not feel isolated from others. They need to feel they are an integral part of the whole class team, yet have the privacy they need to focus.

Individual Work Systems

Help children become and stay organized. Have all materials in the same place at all times. Have a system so that they know what work needs to be done first, what needs to be done next, and what needs to be done after that. Number or color code the system. For example, when children finish their task in box one, they move to box two and continue in this fashion. If children cannot read numbers, get them accustomed to colors. Color boxes are an organized and efficient method to help children complete their tasks. They have three boxes, and the first is red. Children open the red box and complete their task there. When they are finished, they put the task on a tray. They then open the yellow box and complete this task. When they are finished, they put this task on the tray. Finally, they open the green box, remove the task, and complete it. When finished, they put their task on the tray and open each box to make sure they are all empty. They take the tray over to a special place on the teacher's desk, and they are ready to move to a fun activity like a puzzle. This becomes a ritual—a routine that they follow every day. The boxes are organized from left to right in the order that they are to be completed.

Do not assume anything about children completing tasks. Children with ASD need to be shown in a sequential fashion what to do. They need to be shown how to know when a task is finished. This can be as simple a task as "reading" a book. They need to be shown how to remove the book from the book nook, how to open the book, how to hold the book, how to look at the pictures and "pretend read" the book, and then how to replace the book when they are finished.

Visual Systems

Children with ASD process auditory information with difficulty and have more strength in the area of visual-spatial processing (Lincoln, Courchesne, Harms, & Allen, 1995). This means that they do well with pictures. I have had several older children tell me that they think in pictures. Use visual prompts for everything from teaching routines to having smoother transitions (Dettmer, Simpson, Myles, & Ganz, 2000).

Wrist Bands

Make children wristbands and attach small cards with symbols and words to them using Velcro. When children need something, they turn up the appropriate card on their wristband and show it to the teacher. If they want to get something from their cubby, they turn up the card that says the word "cubby" with a picture of a cubby next to it. They go to their teacher and point to the card. If the child wants to go to the bathroom, there is a picture and a word on the card so the teacher can understand what the child wants. This fosters independence and helps children to be able to communicate in a visual manner.

Everyday Needs and Objects

Another way to use pictures is to make pictures of everything you think children may want. Teach children to hand the picture to you—to actually place the picture in your hand. When the child does this, say, "You want the . . . " and hand the child the object requested.

Visual Prompts

Use visual prompts for helping children line up. Make circles or squares out of construction paper and place them on the floor so that they lead toward the door. Teach the children to line up on the construction paper prompts. As children learn where to stand to line up, gradually remove the prompts so that eventually they do not need them at all (Heflin & Alberto, 2001).

Sign Language

Use visual strategies for communication. Teach the children sign language. It gives them a way to both speak and listen. If you do not know sign language, use gestures. Use specific gestures to signal different activities. For example, make the peace sign with your fingers to signal it is time for everyone to stop working and be still.

Concrete Objects

Concrete objects can be used to help children communicate and express themselves. Teach them to hold and squeeze a stress ball when they are angry and upset instead of hitting themselves or others. Have them use a puppet to demonstrate what they want. They take the puppet to the water source when they are thirsty. They take the puppet to the pencil sharpener when they need their pencil sharpened. They can even take their puppet over to another child, and it is a signal that they want to play with that child.

Staying on Task

Keeping children with autism on task can be a challenge. Lengthen the time they are on tasks by ensuring they know something good is coming upon completion of the task (Egel, 1981). This can be something tangible like a sticker, or it can be a highly preferred activity. In order to get to do the highly preferred activity, children have to first do the less preferred activities (Azrin, Vinas, & Ehle, 2007).

Alternate Movement and Sedentary Activities

Plan the day so that a variety of activities are scheduled (Munk & Repp, 1994). Alternate between activities with high levels of movement and activities that are more sedentary (Prizant & Rubin, 1999). Some children need to engage in sensory-arousing activities like jumping and spinning prior to learning. Once finished, they are ready to calm down and learn.

Classroom Arrangement

Arrange the classroom so there are clear boundaries and designations to differentiate areas (Anderson, Campbell, & Cannon, 1994). Establish boundaries by putting visual markers to indicate different areas of the room. Shelves are a good way to divide the room. Keep in mind proximity issues. Some children do not like to be in close proximity to others. These children need additional space so they can focus on what they are doing.

Indirect Lighting

Use of indirect lighting may be more calming to someone with an easily overstimulated visual system. Bring a lamp from home to warm up an area in the room. Be careful to not seat children directly under fluorescent lights.

Individual Learning Styles

When planning the curriculum, always base the activities on the child's individual characteristics, not on the fact that the child has ASD. Make sure materials are motivating. Observe children to see how they learn best. While it is true that children with ASD share some similar characteristics, they still are each unique.

Concrete Teaching

Teach skills in a highly structured, one-to-one format, providing clear and concise instruction. Speak simply and directly. Be concrete rather than abstract. Use short sentences. Begin with verbal prompts and physical guidance and then gradually use less and less guidance as children learn to complete tasks themselves.

Looking for Causes of Inappropriate Behavior

Before getting upset when children misbehave, it's important to understand the reasons behind misbehavior. The misbehaviors may be ways that children "talk" to tell you something is wrong. For example, tantrums can really be a sign that children are angry, or they can also be a signal that children are frightened. Look at what was happening right before the tantrum, and it will become clear. Walk up to the child and acknowledge what is happening. "It looks like you are really scared." Your words become the words that children wish they could say, and this often defuses the tantrum.

I can still remember the first child with autism that I ever had. He had not been diagnosed with ASD. I just knew that something was different. Every time he got upset, he would knock his head against a wall—the same wall every time. I was really frightened that he would hurt himself. Finally, I understood what was happening. He would engage in head-banging every time he got frustrated because he didn't understand my instructions or when he wanted something from one of the other children. I started using my own words for him, "Jonathon, it looks like you don't understand my directions." He stopped and looked at me. I said, "I'll be glad to show you another way to do it. Let's go to over to the table together and I'll show you." He took my hand, we went to the table, and I showed him again—only this time I was very clear in demonstrating how to do the task.

You have to "read" children and situations. Just like you read a whole book to understand the plot and the characters, you need to read children. Look at the child. Is the child trying to tell you something? Is there too much going on in the classroom that is distracting and confusing? Was the child simply trying to get your attention? Once you have read the situation, you will know better how to handle it.

Minimize Waiting

Children who do not have ASD often have a difficult time waiting. Children with autism find it even harder. There are so many sensory stimulations that occur during wait times like standing in line. There are other children all around, some physically touching each other, as well as more noise than usual as children wait. This can all put children on overload. If you cannot totally minimize waiting times, then teach children something they can do that will keep their attention focused while they do wait. You may designate a specific spot for children to stand or something for them to hold in their hands while waiting.

Teaming With Families

Teamwork and consistency are important. The more home training children receive, the better they will function both at home and at preschool. Let families know that you care and that you want to make a difference with their children. They will be happy to know there is someone else who cares. It is not an easy task to be a parent of a child with ASD. Family lives are completely altered anytime there is a child with special needs. Knowing that there is a caring teacher for their children helps foster a sense of hope.

How to Handle Children With Asperger Syndrome

8

Each child is worth the time it takes to transform a life.

—Maryln Appelbaum

Asperger Syndrome (AS), like autism spectrum disorder, is also grouped under pervasive developmental disorders (American Psychiatric Association, 2000). It, too, affects social and communication skills, but it is milder. Children with AS generally have very good language skills in contrast to children with autism spectrum disorder, who may have little to no speech.

CHARACTERISTICS OF ASPERGER SYNDROME

Hans Asperger first described this disorder in 1944, and it was only in 1991 that it was published in English. It is characterized by subtle impairments in three areas of development: social communication, social interaction, and social imagination. All of these are social skills that affect how children with AS are viewed by others. Because their behavior is different, they often seem to be odd and peculiar to other children. It's not uncommon for these children to be the victims of scapegoating, teasing, and bullying.

Just as children with autism spectrum disorder often have obsessions with objects, children with AS may also have an obsessive interest in objects or in subjects ranging from a fascination with cars or electrical systems to enthrallment with world religions or even a television program. They talk incessantly about their obsession.

The behavior of children with AS is often rigid and inflexible (American Psychiatric Association, 2000). They keep doing what they do, regardless of the result. Leonel was a 5-year-old child in Mrs. Kater's class. He had just learned how to make phone calls. Mrs. Kater received a complaint from another parent of a child in the classroom. The parent said that Leonel continuously phoned her son, Matthew, and that she had had enough. She related what had occurred the prior evening. She was just sitting down to dinner when the phone rang. It was Leonel, asking for Matthew. She told him that Matthew was at karate lessons. He said, "OK." She hung up the phone, and before she could even make it back to the dinner table, the phone rang again. It was Leonel, again asking for Matthew. She told him again that Matthew was at karate practice, and again, he said, "OK." She hung up the phone, and he called again and again and again. This is a classic example of rigid and inflexible behavior. Children with AS, like Leonel, are often impulsive and have difficulty holding back a response. They become narrowly focused on one detail, which, in this case, was speaking to Matthew.

Children with AS are different from children with autism in terms of intelligence. Typically, children with AS have normal or even high IQs. They generally begin talking early, and often they have such a rich vocabulary that their parents may think they are gifted (American Psychiatric Association, 2000). Many are so bright that they go on to high levels of achievement as adults, excelling in areas like math and physics.

In social interactions, children with AS may have inappropriate eye contact. They may look away when speaking so that the listener feels a lack of connection. This is complicated by the fact that children with AS typically have difficulty understanding what others are feeling. They generally can't read emotions through body language, facial expression, and voice inflection, so they do not usually understand when someone becomes frustrated, sad, or upset. Even when told what the other person is feeling, children with AS do not understand how to handle what they are hearing. They may talk at length on a subject, rambling on and on, even if their listeners are bored. They don't know the listeners are bored because they can't read this in the other person. Their interests are limited, so they don't have a wide range of subjects about which to communicate. Moreover, if the topic has anything to do with other people and how they are feeling, children with AS are usually totally lost because this involves skills they just do not have—handling emotions. They cannot handle emotions in themselves, and it is even more difficult to handle emotions in others.

At the same time, children with AS are emotionally vulnerable. They want and need friends but do not know how to begin or maintain a

Figure 8.1 Characteristics of Asperger Syndrome

Characteristics of Asperger Syndrome

- Deficits in social interaction

- Lack of emotional reciprocity

- Intellectual abilities in normal or superior range

- Occurs more in males

- Inappropriate eye contact

- Needs sameness

- Limited interests

- May have poor motor skills

- Poor concentration

- Emotionally sensitive and vulnerable

- Often talks at length on some subject of interest

- Does not grasp that others may not be interested in the same conversation

- Limited problem-solving social skills

- Anxiety

- May interrupt or talk over speech of others

- Difficulty understanding feelings in self

- Difficulty understanding feelings in others

relationship. They are especially sensitive to criticism, perhaps because they have often heard criticism about themselves. Anxiety is still another factor that complicates their relationships. They may feel so much anxiety about social interactions that it can cause them to freeze even more when speaking and relating to others. A list of the characteristics of Asperger Syndrome can be found in Figure 8.1.

Bryan, a 4-year-old in Mr. Finch's class, had AS. He was often isolated because other children did not choose to play with him. He didn't make eye contact when he talked to other children. He often rambled on and on about cars. He was fascinated with cars, and he had a collection of cars at home. One morning, Mr. Finch decided to get the attention of all the children in a new way. He blew a whistle. When Bryan heard the whistle, he ran to the wall and hid his head in his arms against the wall. His anxiety level had been high even before he heard the whistle. The whistle put him over the top in anxiety so that all he wanted to do was run and hide. When other children started laughing at him, he felt even more miserable. He felt like he did not fit in. Fortunately, Mr. Finch understood immediately what had happened. He gave the rest of the class something to do to keep them busy. He went over to the wall where Bryan was trying to hide. Mr. Finch spoke very calmly and soothingly to Bryan, assuring him it was safe in the classroom. He took out the whistle and showed it to Bryan. He promised to not blow the whistle in the classroom anymore.

In this case, an object produced the anxiety, but it can also be increased by criticism and harsh words. Some children do not run over to a wall and hide; rather, they hide inside themselves feeling scared and anxious. These children need help and understanding so they can relax and feel good about themselves and the classroom.

STRATEGIES FOR SUCCEEDING WITH CHILDREN WITH AS

Calm, Predictable Routine

Change is frightening for all children, and children with AS may find it even more daunting. They need to be slowly prepared for all changes. Tell them ahead of time if there will be shifts in the routine so they can be emotionally prepared. Warn ahead of transitions, even if they are part of a predictable routine. Use words like, "In five minutes, it will be time to put your work away and get ready for lunch."

If you know ahead that you will be absent and there will be a substitute teacher, inform your children. Tell them the routine they will be following the day the substitute is there.

Be consistent in not only your routine, but in what you say. When you say something, follow through. Consistency is essential for children with AS.

Maintaining Calm

All children take their cues from you, but children with AS do it even more. They may not understand what you are feeling when you are upset, but they know something is different. Fear of the unknown can create even more anxiety.

Engaging Teaching

Make learning fun. The more fun children are having, the less they will feel anxiety. Start all new projects with an introduction that makes children excited. Just as a good meal begins with an appetizer, give them an educational appetizer. Tell them what they will be doing in a way that whets their appetites and makes them want to get involved.

Chunking Lessons

Break lessons into smaller chunks so that children are not over-whelmed. The higher their anxiety, the less they can accomplish. When one chunk is completed, children take a breather and then go on to the next chunk. The breather can be a fun activity. A short break in which they do something else that is still part of the learning assignment can provide relief from working intensely. This means that children need more time for completion of tasks, but it is so worth the time.

Clear, Brief Instructions

Make sure that children understand what they are to do before they do it. Have them check for understanding by repeating the instructions back to a learning buddy or to you.

Caution in Speech

Be very cautious how you talk to children if they are doing a lesson incorrectly. Remember, they are especially sensitive to criticism. Even when you are tactful, they may interpret it as criticism, so choose your words carefully. Keep your focus on telling them what you want them to do rather than telling them what they did wrong. You can simply say, "Here's another way to do this." This keeps it a more positive social interaction.

Observation

Step in if children seem to be having any difficulty so that they don't become overwhelmed. Walk around as children are in their learning centers or doing projects and stop to help children who need help. This is an effective strategy for all of your children and is especially useful for children with AS.

Children's Interests

Take advantage of children's obsessive interests whenever you can by incorporating them into the lessons. For example, if a child is fixated on cars and the class is learning about shapes, the child can show other children the round wheels on a car.

Proactively Protecting Children

Children with AS are often the victims of teasing and bullying. They need to be protected, and the best way to do this is to teach children to honor the diversity of others.

Commonalities Rather Than Differences

Do exercises with the class so that all children are more accepting of each other. A powerful exercise is the "things in common" exercise. Children typically look for differences in all children and single out children who are different from others for teasing. Break the class into groups of approximately five or six. Appoint a leader in each group who will report the results from that group's exercise back to the rest of the class. Have children face each other and instruct them that they have a couple of minutes to find things they have in common. Give them some examples like they all come to preschool and they all wear shoes. Give them a one-minute warning so they know when it is nearly time to be finished. Have the children tell the class what they have in common. When they are finished, have children within the group turn to their neighbors on each side and tell the children one thing they like about them.This is a great bonding activity that keeps children focused on what they have in common rather than what is different. It changes the whole tone of the classroom, as children start looking for things they have in common rather than differences.

Classroom Posters

Children are affected by their environment. Have posters in the room that foster caring. The more they see the signs, the more the signs become part of the classroom culture. Have posters that show children holding hands, children sharing, and children helping other children.

Teaching Social Skills

Children with AS typically do not have appropriate social skills. They need to be taught these skills (Cumine, Dunlop, & Stevenson, 2005). This includes how to ask for what they want and how to say thank you when they receive it. They need to learn how to ask if they can share toys and how to tell other children in kind ways they don't want to play with them. All children need to learn these skills, but children with AS need them even more. These skills do not come naturally. Rehearse with children over and over again until they understand and can do it easily. You can also use stories to teach social skills. Have them role-play different parts of stories and practice using skills.

Being a Matchmaker

Seating is important. Seat children near you at different times during the day when you think they may need some extra reassurance. Act like a matchmaker, assigning children to be buddies with children with AS. Make sure the children you appoint are supportive, caring, and enjoy helping others. The goal is for them to become classroom pals.

Stopping Obsessive Talk

When children with AS continuously talk about a topic on which they are fixated, other children can become annoyed. This creates social problems for the child with AS. Restrict the talk about the obsessive topic to a specific time of day. If the child starts talking about the obsession at another time, remind the child that there is a special time for talking about this topic. If the child talks on and on about the topic, change the subject in a gentle but firm manner. "Chase, you can talk about this later. Right now, let's all talk about. . . . " You can also use visual cues like holding up a stop sign. Children learn that when they see the visual cue, it's time to stop talking.

Stress Reduction

Because anxiety is high, it's important to teach children how to relax. Teach children appropriate anxiety reduction tools like deep breathing and counting to five to use when feeling stressed.

Comforting Object

There are some things that even adults find comforting. After my mom passed away, I liked putting her blanket on my bed. It gave me comfort and was a constant reminder of my mom. Some adults wear religious symbols because it makes them feel better. Many adults have different types of comforting objects. Once as I was standing in line for airport security, I saw a woman holding a stuffed bear and cuddling it. It was shortly after 9/11 and many travelers needed comfort. Children need comforting objects too. Some children have a favorite stuffed animal that helps them feel better.

I often recommend that children bring a photo of someone that is comforting. Some children from broken homes will bring photos of the absent parent. The photo needs to be put into a small container like a little pill bottle or laminated so that it can be carried in their pockets. When children feel anxious, they get out their photo and look at it. The photo can also be on their cubby. Children can go and stand by their cubbies and look at the photo until they feel better.

Relaxing Pictures

Visual pictures work well for stress reduction too. Have a set of relaxing pictures. They can include a sunset, the beach, the mountains, or other relaxing scenes. Involve children in helping you choose the relaxation scenes. When children are stressed, they choose a relaxation picture and look at it while deep breathing until they feel better.

Provide regular breaks during the day to engage in fun activities (Cumine et al., 2005). A short, regularly scheduled break can alleviate stress and help the children to focus better. During these breaks, it is good to provide movement activities like stretching or singing fun songs.

Dare to Dream

Above all, when you are working with children with AS, have hope and patience. Be patient as you talk and listen to these children. Help them to feel they are a part of your classroom. Never underestimate the influence you have in their lives. Believing in them and taking time to connect and show you care can impact not only their present lives, but also their future lives. Teach them to dare to dream, to use the gifts they have to achieve all they can. Talk to them about people like Albert Einstein, who some believe had AS, who did succeed, and who did make a difference (Rowe, 2003). Offer them hope and caring. You are a difference maker.

How to Handle Children With Tourette Syndrome and Obsessive-Compulsive Disorder

9

A happy face comes from a happy heart. A happy heart comes knowing you are building better tomorrows for children.

—Maryln Appelbaum

CHARACTERISTICS OF TOURETTE SYNDROME (TS)

Tourette Syndrome is a neurological disorder characterized by tics (American Psychiatric Association. 2000). These are involuntary, rapid, sudden movements that occur repeatedly in the same way. There are two types of tics: motor tics and vocal tics. Motor tics are movements of the body that range from eye blinking to head jerking to abnormal body jerking. The second type of tics is vocal tics, which can range from throat clearing and belching to odd noises and speaking obscenities. The tics may occur many times a day nearly every day or intermittently. See a list of the types of tics in Figure 9.1.

Tics typically begin with something much less severe like blinking, sniffing, or even cracking knuckles. Children may go through periods in which symptoms are continuously present and other times when all symptoms disappear for weeks or even months. They may feel relieved and think that they are permanently gone. It can be traumatic when they repeatedly return. It's like being on a roller coaster. They feel on top of their own world when the tics are gone, and then they come crashing back down when the tics return.

Figure 9.1 Different Types of Tics

Different Types of Tics
Motor Tics

- Eye blinking
- Eye rolling
- Squinting
- Head jerking
- Facial grimacing or contortions
- Nose twitching
- Body jerking
- Hitting self or others
- Clapping
- Kissing hand or others
- Pinching
- Leg jerking
- Shoulder shrugging
- Knee knocking
- Stooping
- Jumping or hopping
- Kicking
- Stomping
- Ankle flexing
- Table banging
- Picking at lint
- Lip pouting
- Lip licking
- Lip smacking
- Tongue thrusting
- Mouth opening
- Hair tossing or twisting
- Arm flapping, flailing, or jerking
- Arm squeezing
- Smelling fingers and objects
- Shivering
- Abdominal jerking
- Throwing things
- Tearing books
- Tearing paper
- Tearing cloth
- Squatting
- Skipping
- Stepping backwards
- Walking on toes
- Twirling in circles
- Knee bending
- Foot tapping or shaking
- Foot dragging
- Chewing or pulling on clothes
- Somersaults
- Body slamming
- Scratching

Simple Vocal Tics

- Throat clearing
- Grunting
- Sniffling
- Belching
- Spitting
- Snorting
- Squeaking
- Hiccupping
- Coughing
- Humming
- Yelling
- Puffing
- Sucking
- Whistling
- Honking or hissing
- Laughing
- Screaming
- Shouting
- Yelping
- Barking
- Moaning
- Saying unintelligible noises

• Saying words like "wow" or "hey"	• Calling out
• Guttural sounds	• Squealing
• Noisy breathing	• Clicking or clacking
• Gurgling	• Making "tsk" and "pft" noises

Complex Vocal Tics

• Repeating of phrases	• Repeating one's own words
• Repeating words	• Repeating others' words, echolalia
• Repeating parts of words	
• Animal sounds	
• Stuttering	• Speaking obscenities or socially taboo phrases
• Amplitude of speech	
• Talking to oneself	

Children with TS do have times when they have some control over their symptoms. This can last for a few seconds to hours at a time; however, when they suppress them, they may be merely postponing even more severe tics. Children will say, "I have to do it!" They eventually have to express them and may become very embarrassed. They do not like to feel like they are different from other children.

Tics occur more frequently when children are stressed. They generally decrease when children are more relaxed or when they are concentrating on something that totally absorbs their interest. Jeremy started having symptoms when he was only 3 years old. His parents had just had a new baby. His teacher noticed that he blinked his eyes repeatedly. A few months later, he was absent with the flu for several days. He was home with the new baby and saw how often the baby was held all day. When he returned to preschool, he cleared his throat over and over and blinked his eyes repeatedly.

CHARACTERISTICS OF OBSESSIVE-COMPULSIVE DISORDER (OCD)

Obsessive-Compulsive Disorder (OCD) is a neurological disorder characterized by involuntary, recurrent obsessions and compulsions (American Psychiatric Association, 2000). These create anxiety, take up lots of time, and interfere with normal functioning. Obsessions are persistent thoughts, images, ideas, or feelings that children have. Everyone now and then may have persistent thoughts, images, and ideas, but these are excessive and generally do not make sense. The thoughts are so severe that children become frozen and can't do anything. They are literally stuck within their thoughts.

Figure 9.2 Obsessions

Obsessions

- Focusing on cleanliness
- Focusing on exactness
- Needing to remember something
- Focusing on minor details over and over again
- Overfocusing on one idea or action
- Focusing on the rightness or wrongness of a situation
- Focusing on specific numbers
- Focusing on certain colors for certain situations
- Being preoccupied with sensations that can include burning or cutting self
- Focusing on knives and scissors
- Extreme anxiety about harming self
- Extreme worry about harming others
- Worrying that something terrible is going to happen
- Overfocusing on germs and illness
- Focusing on foods and eating
- Focusing on forbidden acts and behaviors
- Worrying about aggressive impulses and images
- Focusing on behaviors that are forbidden

Compulsions are repetitive, ritualistic behaviors that are usually associated with the obsession. Children engage in the compulsions to relieve the tension, stress, and anxiety that are associated with the obsessive thinking. A huge majority of children with TS also have OCD.

OCD behaviors may increase and decrease, depending on stress due to events in the lives of children. These events may be emotional, physical, or environmental and are anxiety-inducing. Children become stuck and find it hard to function at different times. See Figures 9.2 and 9.3 for more characteristics of OCD.

PSYCHOLOGICAL CONSEQUENCES OF TS AND OCD

Serious issues can arise in children who have TS, OCD, or both. Children may have problems arriving at preschool on time because they are so busy at home with rituals (Purcell, 1999). They may be obsessed with perfection in projects and tasks. This obsession can cause them to do and redo whatever they are working on. A simple painting can take a long time because it is done over and over again. They may become embarrassed by

Figure 9.3 Compulsions

Compulsions

- Checking and rechecking amount of money
- Checking and rechecking if door is closed and windows shut
- Checking and adjusting clothes
- Aligning objects so they are a certain way
- Counting objects in a room
- Counting squares of sidewalk
- Walking without stepping on cracks in sidewalk
- Counting to a certain number prior to action
- Repeating actions over and over again
- Brushing hair a certain number of strokes
- Finishing a task once it is begun, even if time involved is excessive
- Inability to switch activities
- Repeating the actions others already did
- Repeating sounds and words to self
- Repeating numbers to self
- Asking the same question over and over again
- Concern with doing things perfectly
- Fear of harm coming to a loved one
- Picking sores, skin, nose
- Sucking thumb or fingers
- Biting nails
- Cutting self
- Repeatedly cracking knuckles
- Smelling self or objects
- Excessive hand washing, bathing, cleaning
- Drawing or writing over and over again until paper looks perfect

---

their own behaviors. It is not a good feeling to feel different from others, so children with OCD often try to hide their rituals and thoughts from others. They may become angry or depressed and discouraged and feel like they are different. This leads to even more discouragement and hopelessness. It also increases anxiety, which can increase their symptoms even more.

Their relationships with others may be impaired because of their symptoms and also because of their own oversensitivity and social embarrassment. It can cause them to go through periods of withdrawal from others. Self-esteem and self-confidence are lowered, and feeling unloved and frustrated is increased. It becomes a cycle of despair because the worse they feel, the more anxious they become, and the more anxious they become, the more their symptoms increase, creating further embarrassment.

STRATEGIES FOR SUCCEEDING WITH CHILDREN WITH TS AND OCD

Transition Warnings

Children with OCD cannot easily change tasks. They may have to complete the previous task before they can go on to the next one. Give them lots of advanced notice of transitions and shifts in activities. "In ten minutes, we will be going outside. Start to put everything away because it all has to be finished by then."

Structured Routine

Structure, routine, and consistency are recurrent themes throughout this book. Children need to know what will happen and when it will happen. A regular routine helps children realize that A follows B. They know what to expect, and it helps them stay on task.

Group Projects

Help children not stay isolated (Purcell, 1999). Because they feel embarrassed and often secretive about their compulsions and tics, children tend to isolate. Assign group projects so that children get to meet and mingle with others.

Teaching Coping Strategies

You will have to adjust your expectations for children with OCD. This is a very real disability. Children may have to engage in a compulsive act over and over again before they finish it. As long as you know this ahead of time, you can be prepared. For example, some children with OCD have a phobia of germs. They need to wash their hands over and over again. Their hands may become raw from so much hand washing; however, they still need to wash their hands.

Chelsie had OCD and TS. Mrs. Carlyle, her teacher, observed that Chelsie washed her hands continually. She observed that every time Chelsie used play objects, she always washed her hands afterward. One day, she noticed that while Chelsie was in the dramatic play area, she stopped what she was doing five times to go to the sink and wash her hands. Mrs. Carlyle also noticed that Chelsie washed her hands a lot if another child was coughing or sneezing. She washed her hands after she touched any foreign object like the door. Mrs. Carlyle spoke to a friend who was a school nurse and asked her if she had any ideas. The school nurse recommended a brand of disinfectant that Chelsie could carry in her pocket and use whenever she wanted to wash her hands. Mrs. Carlyle met with Chelsie and told her that she had observed that a lot of time was spent in hand washing. She asked her if she would like another easier, quicker way to have clean hands. Chelsie readily agreed, so Mrs. Carlyle explained how the disinfectant worked and asked her if she wanted one. Chelsie said, "Yes," and from that moment on in the classroom, she used her hand disinfectant. Chelsie still had OCD and TS, but she had learned a new way to manage her behavior.

Class Task Assists

Children with OCD may need extra time on task (Purcell, 1999). It takes them longer to complete tasks because of the fact that they are often compelled to check and recheck what they did. This means that they may get less done than other children. Make sure that children do not feel pressured to do too much. Children can become so frustrated when they feel overwhelmed that they stop and do nothing. In this case, less is definitely more. Less to do can help children get more accomplished.

Seating

Do not seat children with TS in front of other children if they have severe tics. That can cause profound embarrassment for children. Seat children where they can still see and hear you yet will not feel like others are staring at them.

De-Stressing

Stress is a major component in symptoms. It is important to recognize that children with both TS and OCD need to have ways to de-stress. The less stress and anxiety they feel, the more they can get done.

Have a safe place for children to relax when they feel stressed. Use the relaxation station described in Chapter 4 for those times when children are feeling extreme stress. When they go there for a few minutes, it eases the stress so they can be comfortable within the classroom.

Movement helps decrease stress. Ensure that children have outdoor time. Never ground children from having their special times for exercise.

Signals

When children are stuck in a ritual and cannot get unstuck, have a signal they can give for you to help them (Purcell, 1999). For example, they may have a special card in their pockets with a blue circle. Whenever they are stuck and want help, they take the card out of their pockets and put it where you can see it. It's a signal for you to help them and also a way for them to alleviate stress.

Pro-Social Activities

Children with TS often feel isolated because of the stigma of having tics. Help to reduce these feelings by having peer partner activities and setting up a pro-social classroom in which diversity is honored (Carter & O'Donnell, 2000).

Understanding the Disorder

Be empathetic to the needs of children with TS and OCD. The more you understand how they feel, the better you will be able to accommodate them. For example, you may get angry when you think a child with TS is not listening. That child may be thinking, "My throat is clearing over and over again, and my eyes are blinking. The teacher has called on me and gets mad because she thinks I'm not listening." In reality, the child is so busy focusing on the tics that it is hard for the child to hear what you are saying. Still another child with OCD may be thinking, "I can't think about what Mrs. Jennings is saying. I am seeing an image over and over in my head of me getting ill if I don't get up and wash my hands. I have to sit here instead and listen, but I can't think about anything else. I sure can't focus on what is happening in class."

When children are feeling like this, it is nearly impossible for them to do what you ask. You can get their attention, but first you will have to help them relax. They cannot simply stop their minds. These are both real disorders. Medication will help, but it cannot take the place of an understanding teacher. Talk to children in mini-conferences and ask them to think of ways they can focus more clearly. Many children have learned their own little tricks to help. Some children carry stress balls. Some wash their hands over and over again with disinfectant without standing up.

Some have learned deep breathing. Some have a mantra they say over and over again to themselves until they feel calm and in control. For some children, help comes in the form of medical treatment and medication. But for all children, a caring teacher to help them on days when they feel out of control can change a rainy day inside that child's mind to sunshine. You are a difference maker.

Conclusion

I hope this book has made a difference in your life. More than that, I hope it makes a difference in the lives of every child you teach. I want you to know how important you are. You truly are a difference maker. This poem is my concluding gift to you. It is called "You Believed in Me." As you read it, think about the hard-to-handle children you have had in your classes. This could be what any of them may one day write to you.

> REMEMBER ME.
> I am the one who caused you to have grey hairs.
> I am the one who was your greatest challenge.
> I am the one who was angry, defiant, difficult,
> But even on my worst days,
> YOU BELIEVED IN ME.
> You knew that even though I was tough on the outside,
> Inside, I needed you.
> YOU BELIEVED IN ME.
> I was ashamed because I couldn't control myself.
> I was embarrassed because I knew I was different from everyone else.
> I felt dumb, backwards, stupid, bad,
> But on the outside—I sauntered, I talked back, I created disruptions.
> But still, YOU BELIEVED IN ME.
> And now, years later, I am taking this time
> To tell you that because you saw through my behavior,
> You did what changed my life forever:
> You turned me from an angry, defiant child into who I am today.
> YOU BELIEVED IN ME.
> I graduated school instead of being a dropout.
> I went on to achieve a wonderful career.
> I am married and a parent.
> I am a respected member of my community.
> I try each day to give back what you gave me.
> YOU BELIEVED IN ME and gave me hope.
> THANK YOU.

And that is what you do for your students. You believe in them and give them hope.

References

Allen, J. P., Hauser, S. T., & Borman-Spurrell, E. (1996). Attachment theory as a framework for understanding sequelae of severe adolescent psychopathology: An 11-year follow-up study. *Journal of Consulting and Clinical Psychology, 64,* 254–263.

American Psychiatric Association. (2000). *Diagnostic and statistical manual of mental disorders* (4th ed.). Washington, DC: Author.

Anderson, C. A., & Bushman, B. J. (2001). Effects of violent video games on aggressive behavior, aggressive cognition, aggressive affect, physiological arousal, and prosocial behavior: A meta-analytic review of the scientific literature. *Psychological Science, 12,* 353–359.

Anderson, S. R., Campbell, S., & Cannon, B. O. (1994). The May Center for Early Childhood Education. In S. L. Harris & J. S. Handleman (Eds). *Preschool education programs for children with autism* (pp. 15–36). Austin, TX: PRO-ED.

Appelbaum, M. (2008). *The one-stop guide to RTI: Academic and behavioral interventions.* Thousand Oaks, CA: Corwin Press.

Azrin, N. H., Vinas, V., & Ehle, C. T. (2007). Physical activity as reinforcement for classroom calmness of ADHD children: A preliminary study. *Child & Family Behavior Therapy, 29*(2), 1–8.

Bagdi, A., & Pfister, I. K. (2006). Childhood stressors and coping actions: A comparison of children and parents' perspectives. *Child and Youth Care Forum, 35*(1), 21–40.

Banks, R. (1997). *Bullying in schools.* Eric Digest. Eric-RIEO, 19970401.

Bausman, K., Bent, S., & Collister, J. (1999). *Improving social skills at the elementary and secondary level.* ERIC, 62 pp. (ED433099)

Beane, A. (1999). Fostering a bully-free classroom. *Curriculum Review, 39,* 4.

Bettmann, J. (2000). Nurturing the respectful community through practical life. *NAMTA Journal, 25*(1), 101–116.

Biederman, J., Mick, E., Faraone, S. V., Spencer, T., Wilens, T. E., & Wozniak, J. (2000). Pediatric mania: A developmental subtype of bipolar disorder? *Biological Psychiatry, 48,* 458–466.

Bowman, R., Carr, T., Cooper, K., Miles, R., & Toner, T. (1998). *Innovative Strategies for Unlocking Difficult Children.* Chapin, SC: YouthLight, Inc.

Brown, M. S., Ilderton, P., Taylor, A., & Lock, R. H. (2001). Include a student with an attention problem in the General Education Classroom. *Intervention in School & Clinic, 34*(1), 50–53.

Bullies and their victims. (2001). *Harvard Mental Health Letter, 18,* 4–7.

Carney, A. G., & Merrell, K. W. (2001). Bullying in schools: Perspectives on understanding and preventing an international problem. *School Psychology International, 22,* 364–382.

Carroll, A., Houghton, S., Taylor, M., Hemingway, F., List-Kerz, M., Cordin, R., et al. (2006). Responding to interpersonal and physically provoking situations in classrooms: Emotional intensity in children with attention deficit hyperactivity disorder. *International Journal of Disability, Development & Education, 53*(2), 209–227.

Carter, A. S., & O'Donnell, D. A. (2000). Social and emotional adjustment in children affected with Gilles de la Tourette's syndrome: Associations with ADHD and family functioning. *Journal of Child Psychology & Psychiatry & Allied Disciplines, 41*(2), 215–223.

Charney, R. S. (1998). Got the "kids who blurt out" blues? *Instructor-Intermediate, 107*(6), 90–93.

Cumine, V., Dunlop, J., & Stevenson, G. (2005). *Asperger Syndrome, a practical guide for teachers.* London: David Fulton Publishers.

Denson, T. F., Pedersen, W. C., & Miller, N. (2006). The displaced aggression questionnaire. *Journal of Personality & Social Psychology, 90*(6), 1032–1051.

Dess, N. K. (2001). Saved by the bell? Serious science brings hope to victims and bullies. *Psychology Today, 34*(6) 47.

Dettmer, S., Simpson, I., Myles, B. S., & Ganz, J. B. (2000). The use of visual supports to facilitate transitions of students with autism. *Focus on Autism and Other Developmental Disabilities, 15*, 163–169.

Duffy, A. (2007). Does bipolar disorder exist in children: A selected review. *Canadian Journal of Psychiatry, 52*(7), 409–417.

Egel, A. (1981). Reinforcer variation: Implications for motivating developmentally disabled children. *Journal of Applied Behavior Analysis, 14*, 345–350.

Ferko, D. K. (2005). Proactively address challenging behaviors. *Intervention in School & Clinic, 41*(1), 30–31.

Fine, L. (2002). Study: Minimum ADHD incidence is 7.5 percent. *Education Week, 21*(28), 10.

Frank, K. (2001). *ADHD: 102 practical strategies for "reducing the deficit."* Chapin, SC: YouthLight, Inc.

Gartrell, D. (2007). Tattling: It drives teachers bonkers. *Young Children, 62*(1), 46–48.

Gillberg, C. (2003). ADHD and DAMP: A general health perspective. *Child & Adolescent Mental Health, 8*(3), 106–113.

Gunter, P. L., & Shores, R. E. (1995). On the move: Using teacher/student proximity to improve students' behavior. *Teaching Exceptional Children, 28*(1), 12–15.

Hallam, S., Price, J., & Katsarou, G. (2002). The effects of background music on primary school pupils' task performance. *Educational Studies, 28*(2), 111–122.

Harris, K. R., Friedlander, B. D., Saddler, B., Frizzelle, R., & Graham, S. (2005). Self-monitoring of attention versus self-monitoring of academic performance: Effects among students with ADHD in the General Education classroom. *Journal of Special Education, 39*(3), 145–156.

Heflin, L. J., & Alberto, P. A. (2001). Establishing a behavioral context for learning for students with autism. *Focus on Autism & Other Developmental Disabilities, 16*, 93–102.

Heydenberk, W., & Heydenberk, R. (2007). More than manners: Conflict resolution in primary level classrooms. *Early Childhood Education Journal, 35*(2), 119–126.

Hipsky, S. (2007). Differentiated instruction: Flexibility without breaking. *Essays in Education, 19*, 96–99.

Jenson, E. (2000). *Brain-based learning.* San Diego, CA: Brain Store, Inc.

Jepson, B. (2007). *Changing the course of autism: A scientific approach for parents and physicians.* Boulder, CO: Sentient Publications.

Jimenez, K. (2000). Is your child more than a handful? *Pediatrics for Parents, 18*, 3–4.

Kemp, K. A., & Eaton, M. A. (2008). *RTI: The classroom connection for literacy: Reading intervention and measurement.* Port Chester, NY: Dude Publishing.

Kendall, P. C., & Treadwell, K. R. H. (2007). The role of self-statements as a mediator in treatment for youth with anxiety disorders. *Journal of Consulting & Clinical Psychology, 75*(3), 380–389.

Leslie, L. K., Weckerly, J., Plemmons, D., Landsyerk, J., & Eastman, S. (2004). Implementing the American Academy of Pediatrics Attention-Deficit/Hyperactivity Disorder diagnostic guidelines in primary care settings. *Pediatrics, 114*(1), 129–140.

Lincoln, A. J., Courchesne, E., Harms, L., & Allen, M. (1995). Sensory modulation of auditory stimuli in children with autism and receptive developmental language disorder: Event-related brain potential evidence. *Journal of Autism and Developmental Disorders, 25,* 521–539.

Mukaddes, N. M., Bilge, S., Alyanak, B., Kora, M. E. (2000). Clinical characteristics and treatment responses in cases diagnosed as Reactive Attachment Disorder. *Child Psychiatry & Human Development, 30*(4), 273–287.

Munk, D. D., & Repp, A. C. (1994). The relationship between instructional variables and problem behavior: A review. *Exceptional Children, 60,* 390–401.

National Joint Committee on Learning Disabilities. (2007). Learning disabilities and young children: Identification and intervention. *Learning Disability Quarterly, 30*(1), 63–72.

Overstreet, S. (2000). Exposure to community violence: Defining the problem and understanding the consequences. *Journal of Child & Family Studies, 9*(1), 7–25.

Parish, T., & Mahoney, S. (2006). Classrooms: How to turn them from battlegrounds to connecting places. *Education, 126*(3), 437–440.

Parker, H. C. (2005). *The ADHD handbook for schools: Effective strategies for identifying and teaching students with attention-deficit/hyperactivity disorder.* Plantation, FL: Specialty Press, Inc.

Prizant, B. M., & Rubin, E. (1999). Contemporary issues in interventions for autism spectrum disorders: A commentary. *JASH, 24,* 199–208.

Purcell, J. (1999). *Children, adolescents, and obsessive compulsive disorder in the classroom.* ERIC, 22 pp. (ED445439)

Reiter, J. (2004). Recognizing and treating adults with attention deficit hyperactivity disorder. *Psychiatric Times, 21*(Supplement), 1–4.

Rowe, C. (2003). Albert Einstein, Andy Kaufman, and Andy Warhol: The controversial disorder they may have shared. *Biography, 7*(12), 86–114.

Schwartz, E. (2006). Reactive Attachment Diorder: Implications for school readiness and school functioning. *Psychology in the Schools, 43*(4), 471-479.

Skinner, C. H., Cashwell, T. H., & Skinner, A. L. (2000). Increased tootling: The effects of a peer-monitored group contingency program on students' reports of peers' prosocial behaviors. *Psychology in the Schools, 37*(3), 263–271.

Smith, S. (2001). Stephen W. Smith: Strategies for building a positive classroom environment by preventing behavior problems. *Intervention in School & Clinic, 37,* 31–36.

Sprung, B., Froschi, M., & Hinitz, B. (2005). *The anti-bullying and teasing book for preschool classrooms.* Beltsville, MD: Gryphon House.

Stearns, C., Dunham, M., McIntosh, D., & Dean, R. S. (2004). Attention deficit hyperactivity disorder and working memory in clinically referred adults. *International Journal of Neuroscience, 114*(2), 273–287.

Stolzer, J. M. (2007). The ADHD epidemic in America. *Ethical Human Psychology & Psychiatry, 9*(2), 109–116.

Stuart, S. K., Flis, L. D., & Rinaldi, C. (2006). Connecting with families: Parents speak up about preschool services for their children with autism spectrum disorders. *Teaching Exceptional Children, 39*(1), 46–51.

Turnuklu, A. (2007). Students' conflicts: Causes, resolution strategies, and tactics in high schools. *Educational Administration: Theory & Practice, 49,* 159–166.

Valas, H. (2001). Learned helplessness and psychological adjustment II: Effects of learning disabilities and low achievement. *Scandinavian Journal of Educational Research, 45*(2), 101–114.

Wagner, C. (1985). *Color power*. Chicago: Wagner Institute for Color Research.

Walker, M. (1991). *The power of color*. New York: Avery Publishing Group.

Winebrenner, S. (2006). *Teaching kids with learning difficulties in the regular classroom: Ways to challenge and motivate struggling students to achieve proficiency with required standards*. Minneapolis, MN: Spirit Press.

Woods, C. S. (2003). Phoemic awareness: A crucial bridge to reading. *Montessori Life, 15*(2), 37–39.

Index

CORWIN PRESS

The Corwin Press logo—a raven striding across an open book—represents the union of courage and learning. Corwin Press is committed to improving education for all learners by publishing books and other professional development resources for those serving the field of PreK–12 education. By providing practical, hands-on materials, Corwin Press continues to carry out the promise of its motto: **"Helping Educators Do Their Work Better."**

Appelbaum Training Institute (ATI) provides the latest, the best, and the most research-based information on the most current subjects in a fun and enjoyable manner through professional development, training, and resources to educators and parents of children of all ages and diverse backgrounds. The ATI motto is **"Building Bridges to the Future,"** and that is exactly what the Appelbaum Training Institute does every day in every way for educators across the world.